Y0-AEV-982

WOMEN AND THE FOOD CYCLE

HD
6073
.F7
W65x

WOMEN AND THE FOOD CYCLE

Introduction by Marilyn Carr

Intermediate Technology Publications 1989

GOSHEN COLLEGE LIBRARY
GOSHEN, INDIANA

Intermediate Technology Publications, 103/105 Southampton
Row, London WC1B 4HH, UK

© This selection United Nations Development Fund for
Women 1989

ISBN 1 85339 055 0

Printed by the Russell Press Ltd, Gamble Street, Nottingham
NG7 4ET, UK. Telephone: (0602) 784505

CONTENTS

5-9-90 NUT/JB

FROM HAND TO MOUTH

An Introduction by Marilyn Carr

Every day, in millions of villages in the Third World, hundreds of tonnes of grains, grain legumes, starchy roots, seeds, fruit and vegetables are processed for sale into a variety of foodstuffs and drinks. Meat and fish products are also often treated in some way before consumption or sale. There are two good reasons for engaging in this activity. First, without some sort of processing, much fresh produce would perish and be wasted before it could be eaten or sold. Second, most processing techniques add significantly to the value of the foodstuff because they convert the raw material into ready-to-use foods (rice rather than paddy, gari instead of cassava, cooking oil rather than oil seeds) and/or they may improve the flavour of the food in some way (fish may be smoked, for example).

This traditional food processing 'industry' is characterized by its local markets, its small scale, its simple technologies and its low labour productivity. It forms the basis of gainful employment for millions of rural people around the world mainly working part-time within their own households. It often provides the main source of income for poor women, many of whom have total responsibility for the welfare of their families.

Although food processing probably ranks as the major productive activity carried out at the village level, its informal, part-time nature means it is usually overlooked at the level of official statistics. A recent UNIDO report estimated that the industry accounted for only one-fifth of manufacturing activities in developing countries and, in countries such as India, food industries were recorded as employing only eleven per cent of the total labour force.[1] How different would the picture be if all productive activity, formal and informal, were to be counted?

Traditional industries under pressure

Partly as a result of their 'invisibility', the potential of the traditional food processing industries in contributing to national economic development has been largely overlooked. In most countries, plans for the food processing sector consist mainly of

1

establishing modern factory complexes to provide high quality produce and to make the maximum use of available raw materials. Other factories are established to produce non-traditional foods and drinks, often based on imported raw materials.

The millions of people who depend for a living on the processing of food receive little, if any, assistance with their enterprises and are, in fact, losing their hold on this activity as a result of the establishment of capital-intensive manufacturing plants. Stories of the disastrous impact of developments of this type are not hard to find. Modern automatic rice mills are displacing thousands of poverty-stricken women employed in the hand pounding of grain in Asia.

Estimates from Bangladesh reveal that each automatic mill destroys 1,000 part-time jobs in the poorest sector of the economy.[2] Oil milling factories and solvent extraction plants employing only a handful of people are established at a time when traditional village industries based on oil processing are struggling to survive. Similarly, in most countries, millions of dollars are invested in 'modern', urban-based breweries, bakeries, crystal sugar plants, and fruit and vegetable canning plants, while thousands of rural producers struggle to compete with the urban-manufactured foodstuffs or are unable to take full advantage of expanding markets because of their lack of access to credit, improved technologies and training. Thus the assumed advantages of economies of scale in the modern food processing industry must be set off against the real disadvantages which these activities create for the rural economy.

Why big is bad

Another fact, often overlooked, is the frequent inability of modern plants to live up to expectations. The Third World is cluttered with food processing complexes which run at a fraction of their capacity.

For example, automatic rice mills in Bangladesh have rarely exceeded a capacity utilization of fifty per cent and can only operate at all as a result of subsidies.[3] In India, modern oil mill complexes operate on average at thirty-five per cent of their capacity.[4] Reasons for this phenomenon vary from country to country but usually include the shortage of raw materials, problems with power supplies and transport difficulties. Many plants change from being expensive, subsidized burdens into equally expensive non-operational white elephants.

2

There are other problems with large capital-intensive plants. The final product is often highly refined and less nutritious than traditional foods, or foods processed in the traditional way. Highly polished rice, white bread, white sugar, lager beer, cornflakes, boiled sweets, and so on have much less nutritional value than products such as hand-pounded rice, maize meal, gur and corn beer. Perhaps the most striking example of the damage that can be caused is the widely acknowledged correlation between the spread over much of Asia of the disease beri-beri and the spread of mechanized rice milling.

One of the factors often put forward in favour of large-scale plants is that they process foods and provide a market for rural produce which might otherwise be wasted, but, sited as they usually are, in major cities or ports, it is often easier and cheaper to import the raw materials than to acquire them locally. Unnecessarily high standards of quality control and a lack of incentive to develop linkages with the rural economy sometimes contribute to this situation. Thus, local vegetable growers can

Pounding palm nuts by hand is a laborious and inefficient way to extract the oil, but rural women in Africa need the income

Cleanliness is critical but is perfectly possible on the small scale

be deprived of even the benefits of selling their unprocessed produce to a thriving urban market.

The case against large-scale processing complexes is a strong one. But if the trend towards large-scale industrialization in the sector has proved to be such a failure, what are the alternatives? One must surely be helping the small producers to retain control of the food-processing industry either by increasing their productivity in processing existing foodstuffs, or by giving them access to the improved technologies, credit and training needed for the production of new food products.

Small is desirable but difficult

As the need for rural off-farm employment opportunities increases, more attention is being given to ways in which local people can use local resources to make saleable items for neighbouring or more distant markets. The most abundantly available resource in rural areas is food (crops, fruits, vegetables and livestock), and an obvious place to start looking for potential projects based on productive activity, is in the processing of such foods.

Rural producers can sometimes be assisted to make a living from food processing simply through the provision of credit to give them access to tools or raw materials. In many cases, however, the traditional technique or technology is no longer sufficiently productive to provide a satisfactory return for the effort expended. Some processes, such as the hand pounding of grains, are so labour-intensive that they cannot possibly compete with mechanized technologies in cost, even if they pay a very low rate of return to labour. Others, such as some traditional methods of fish smoking, are wasteful of fuel and can cope with only limited quantities of fresh produce at any one time. Many income opportunities are lost (and much food wasted or transported out of the area) because the techniques of processing, and the appropriate technologies, are unknown to local people. As a result of these factors, many of the development projects which aim to assist rural people to gain access to income through food processing are based on the introduction of improved techniques and technologies.

While the advantages of projects of this type can be numerous — the provision of jobs for poor people in rural areas, a low capital investment per workplace, the retention of the value added by processing in the rural communities, and the stimulation of local industries to provide the tools, packaging and other inputs to food processing activities — experience indicates that

4

If these women could process their crops, they could earn more and waste less food (Photo: John Isaac/UN)

a great many problems can arise during implementation. There are now a growing number of case studies which evaluate food processing projects and these show some of the more likely pitfalls encountered by project managers.[5]

Projects: problems and promises

Problems encountered in the implementation of food-processing projects include those common to all projects — erratic supplies of raw materials, difficulties in marketing and socio-cultural constraints — as well as some which are specific to projects of this type, such as compliance with health regulations, quality control and perishable supplies.

Since food processing projects are based upon the utilization of locally available crops or livestock, thought is rarely given to problems of raw material supply. Yet experience indicates that supply problems do occur. One project in Ghana which aimed to increase the productivity of women involved in making gari (processed cassava) was so 'successful' that the demand for raw materials far exceeded supplies, and progress was halted until a cassava grower's association was formed and more land was brought under cultivation with the use of a tractor.[6] A problem of a different type was experienced by a group introduced to mango processing in Honduras. Here it was found (during the second year of the project) that mango trees 'rest' every seven years, thus causing an initially thriving enterprise to come to a sudden halt when all the trees, which had been planted together, stopped producing. A further problem is that of a fluctuating supply of perishable raw materials. A food-processing industry may have to operate on a start-stop basis if the crop is only harvested seasonally and the unprocessed material cannot be stored to await processing later.

The marketing of foodstuffs is a major problem, especially when new types of food are being introduced and when the output is aimed at urban or export markets. Thus, when the mango processing project was started, there was initial consumer resistance to a product such as mango puree, which is not a traditional food. In this case, the co-operative members solved the problem themselves by offering very small quantities of puree for sale in biscuit cones for a few pesos. These proved very popular locally and stimulated a demand for the product in large quantities and in more conventional packaging.[7]

Urban consumers and retailers are particularly conscious of the need for high quality, well-packaged food goods. Good packaging is important, not only to gain sales but also to maintain the quality and prevent deterioration of the foodstuff. A potentially valuable project in Bangladesh involving the small-scale production of dessicated coconut using solar dryers, met with severe marketing problems when urban shopkeepers found their initial orders came in cheap plastic packages which became dirty, torn and infested.[8]

Cleanliness is perhaps the most important factor in marketing foodstuffs. Health hazards are a critical factor in projects, as badly processed foods can transmit disease or cause outbreaks of food-poisoning, some types of which are fatal. In addition to the possibly tragic effects on the consumer, the publicity associated with a food-poisoning outbreak could ruin a food-processing project. Government regulations help to keep up standards in this area, since all but the smallest of enterprises must comply with certain standards of hygiene and can be closed down or refused permission to start, if these standards are not met.

Experience has shown that small food industries throughout the Third World can and do comply with such regulations and that, with proper organization, foodstuffs of export quality can be produced in the average rural household. Perhaps the most famous example of this is the Lijjat Pappad Rollers organization in India. This is a remarkable commercial enterprise which operates as a co-operative society and produces pappads (pre-prepared bread dough) for distribution throughout the world. Starting from a small group of founder members in 1959, it now has over 6,000 productive members who can earn anything from Rs.4 to Rs.40 per day for their work. Dough is prepared to a special formula in twenty-one centres throughout India, and is collected by members who roll this out and dry it in their own back yards. Prepared pappads are then taken back to the centres, where they are thoroughly checked and then packaged, labelled and distributed.[9]

The technology upon which a project is based and the way in which it is developed and introduced can also make the difference between success and failure. Experience shows that a project is much more likely to succeed if the intended beneficiaries are consulted about the improved technology during the design phase and if attention is given to creating an improved technology which is similar to existing technologies in its production and use. It will not, therefore, require too great a change in skills, consumer preferences or cultural habits. This may seem obvious enough, but many a project founders because the technology on which it is based is little or no better than the one already available, or is unacceptable in some way.

Many a pilot project has failed to get beyond its trial phase because no thought had been given to how people were to pay for the technology (in other words, there were no credit mechanisms) or how they were to be persuaded or enabled to produce the processing technology on a commercial basis. The first of these problems is usually the easier to overcome, and many food-processing projects now include a credit (usually revolving loan) component, to assist with the purchase of machinery. Persuading producers to set up the commerical production of the new tools and equipment is much more difficult.

One success story involved the need to produce coconut graters in the Caribbean following the successful testing of twelve prototypes. The potential commerical producers were not convinced that a sufficiently large market for such devices existed, especially since the intended users were poor women, who certainly wanted the new grater, but did not necessarily have the cash to buy one. A local development agency began to

Good packaging is essential to prevent wastage and to encourage sales

A successful enterprise in Papua New Guinea produces banana chips

investigate a likely source of funding to finance the large order necessary. The graters would then be sold on to women's groups on a loan basis. Funds were located, an order for 5,000 graters was placed, and commerical production started.[10]

Government policy can either help or seriously hinder the progress and survival of food processing projects. A good example of this comes from Botswana. Here, a small bakery project was successfully begun in a remote area, to supply the local village stores. After about fourteen months, however, bread sales dropped by sixty per cent in less than a week — and continued to fall over the next few months. It appears that this was because of a government decision to establish a large bakery in the capital, Gaborone, which then sold bread throughout eastern Botswana. Consumers switched to this bread because government subsidies and access to bulk supplies of raw materials meant that this bread was slightly cheaper. In addition it was mechanically and more attractively wrapped, and it had a shelf life of five days as opposed to two days.[11] The issue here is one of whether cheap bread is a higher priority than employment, in rural areas.

The way ahead

As more food processing projects are implemented and evaluated, more information is coming to light which can be used to help in the design of future projects. Hopefully past experience will be learned from, so that past mistakes can be avoided and more projects will be successfully implemented.

Small projects are essential in demonstrating that viable alternatives to large-scale food processing factories are available. Each one, however, provides income-earning opportunities for only a handful of people and they are therefore of limited use unless they are widely replicated. As mentioned earlier, modernization and mechanization in the food-processing sector have displaced millions of the rural poor, and especially women, from paid employment. The challenge is to help such people to protect their source of income and to maintain their hold on the industry. The need is for the technologies and methodologies which have been used in successful projects to be repeated on a widespread basis, and for the correct economic and policy environment to be created to allow this to occur.

References

1. UNIDO, *Appropriate Industrial Technology for Food Storage and Processing*, p.7; pp. 75-76, New York, 1979.
2. Ahmad, M., and Jenkins, A., 'Traditional Paddy Husking — an appropriate technology under pressure', *Appropriate Technology*, Vol. 7, No. 2, IT Publications, 1980.
3. *Selected Issues in Rural Employment*, World Bank, Bangladesh, 1983.
4. Harriss, B., and Kelly, C., 'Food Processing: Policy for Rice and Oil Technology in South Asia', p.70, *IDS Bulletin*, Vol. 13, No. 3, 1982.
5. For a survey on such studies see Carr, M., *Blacksmith, Baker, Roofing-sheet maker . . .* , IT Publications, 1984.
6. Date-Bah, Eugenia, 'Rural Women, Their Activities and Technology in Ghana', ILO, WP 87.
7. Fennelly Levy, M., *Bringing Women into the Community Development Process*, SCF, Westport, 1981.
8. MCC, Job Creation Programme, Bangladesh, Report No. 2, 1981-2.
9. Jain, D., 'Pappad Rollers of Lijjat' in Jain, D., *Women's Quest for Power*, Vikas, Delhi.
10. Carr, M., op.cit., pp.24-5.
11. Carr, M., op. cit., pp.33-4.

9

TRADITIONAL PADDY HUSKING — AN APPROPRIATE TECHNOLOGY UNDER PRESSURE

Mohiuddin Ahmad and Andrew Jenkins

Bangladesh has a large population but a very limited land area and scarce capital resources. In order to use the country's vast labour force more effectively, it is important to supply them with more efficient tools and techniques, at low-cost, so that they can produce more. Instead, however, huge sums of money have been spent on mills and other industrial plants which only employ a few workers, but which could destroy the livelihood of many more. If government policies persist, the situation could well worsen.

Let us take the case of post-harvest rice processing. About 70 per cent of all paddy produced in Bangladesh is husked by rural women either in their own homes or other homes nearby. This provides employment and livelihood to millions of poor women. However, mechanical and automatic mills, encouraged by the cheap capital provided by nationalized banks and by subsidized electricity, are gradually taking over the market, increasing unemployment and destitution.

As Bangladesh is unusually fortunate in having such a low-cost, labour-intensive dispersed agro-industry, it is unfortunate that the spread of custom mills, accelerated by rural electrification and the establishment of several new major mills, could rapidly change the situation. In addition, it is unfair that the large numbers of rural women carrying out household manual paddy husking often receive rates of return for their labour which are so low that they are unable to support themselves.

It can be seen from Table 1 that the production costs of milling are very significantly lower for custom mills than for the household method (such as the dheki, illustrated on page 12), which makes mechanical milling a very attractive investment for an entrepreneur. It is made even more attractive by the stimulus provided by cheap electricity, as is recognized in the Power Development Board's Rural Electrification feasibility study which gave the contribution of rice mills to total benefits from rural electrification as 15 per cent.[1]

The benefits of the new technology accrue entirely to two groups:

1. The entrepreneurs drawing profits from their mills with rates of return varying widely, but averaging 70 per cent per annum.
2. The farmers with surplus crops who can dispense with hired female labour and take advantage of the much lower costs of the mills. Small and marginal farmers who traditionally used the labour of their own families for husking largely continue to do so since the cost of the labour is zero, and transport to the mill may be both difficult and costly.

These benefits are entirely paid for by the displacement of large numbers of female labour from the poorest classes. These women either work in the households of the farmers who produced surpluses in the post-harvest period on a wage basis, or buy in paddy individually or collectively, husk it in their own homes and sell it. Recently, a number of women's paddy-husking groups have been organized by IRDP, BRAC and others, with some success.[2] An average mill has a capacity of 0.2 mds/hr. However, most women work part-time, as they have other responsibilities. It can therefore be estimated that one mill displaces about 300 women. Of course, the mill requires labour for parboiling, drying,

The dheki — the traditional paddy-husking device used by women in Bangladesh

winnowing and other related activities, but this labour was also previously required and has not, therefore, been included in the calculations.

In 1977, there were about 7,600 licensed custom mills in Bangladesh, increasing at a rate of 5 to 7 per cent per annum.[3] Taking the lower figure, this gives an annual increase of 380, displacing well over 100,000 women per year. As will be seen from Table 1, the investment/output ratios of the technologies are almost the same, but whereas investment in mills is expensive in foreign exchange in terms of raw materials, spare parts and fuel, investment in local technology has largely been completed. There is a large existing investment in dhekis, which have a very low rate of depreciation, that will be scrapped or highly under-used if custom mills capture the market.

Table 1. Comparative advantages of the different technologies

	Cost per workplace (milling) only	Production cost per md for milling (full processing in brackets)	Profit per md	Investment per unit of output (for milling)
	Taka*	Taka	Taka	Taka
Household	125 (part time)	11.7 (14.7)	—	625
Custom Mill	17,000	1.0 (2.45)	1.0 (3.05)	850

* 34.5 Taka = £1 sterling (30.6.80)

To summarize, the mechanical milling technology is profitable purely because it is labour displacing. Nothing new is created or produced; in fact the quality of dheki-husked rice is generally considered to be higher than that of machine-milled rice. Whilst clearly a profitable activity for the entrepreneur, is mechanical milling a priority for the nation's scarce capital?

Alternative employment for displaced labour

In areas where women have been displaced, available alternatives are begging, unemployment or general domestic employment at half the dheki rate. It seems unlikely that other cottage industries could create jobs at the rate needed to keep up with this rate of displacement as well as taking care of population growth. The increasing rate of landlessness will also increase the pool of labour available. On the other hand, if foodgrain production increased according to government plans at the rate of 4.7 per cent per annum *and* the spread of mechanical mills was restricted, then household paddy-husking could make a very significant contribution to employment. After a certain period when available labour had been absorbed, wages should rise, creating a redistribution effect in favour of the landless class.

The effect of automatic rice mills

At the present time a number of expensive proposals for automatic rice mills are being floated. These rely heavily on imported technology and are on a much larger scale than the custom mills. The only one which has been in operation over a long period is the Comilla Modern Rice Mill which, up to 1977-8, had never run at above about 9 per cent of engineered capacity, and which made substantial losses. There are a number of reasons why this type of mill may be technically unpractical in Bangladesh, including the vulnerability of sophisticated technology to breakdowns, the uncertainties in the supply of raw materials or spares, and failure of management. However, assuming its feasibility, the labour-displacing effect will be even greater than that of custom mills because it will do away with the need for small-scale drying, parboiling, winnowing, etc.

To take an example, the 'Z'-type mill will produce two tons per hour, thus displacing the labour force of nearly three average custom mills. In household-technology terms this would displace 900 part-time women plus another estimated 64 full-timers or about 180 part-timers employed in pre-milling processing. Thus, one automatic rice-mill alone could displace over 1,000 women, providing jobs for 18 skilled and 22 unskilled men at a cost per workplace of Tk 273,000 (skilled) and Tk 224,000 (unskilled).

It is sometimes claimed that there is a shortage of capacity for milling paddy procured by the Food Ministry and therefore investment in automatic mills is required. However, little attempt seems to have been made to compare the possibilities and comparative advantages of the three types of technology available: automatic, custom mill and household technology. Clearly foreign aid donor countries, often themselves manufacturers of automatic rice mills, have a considerable interest in the spread of this technology and particularly in capturing the profitable spare parts business. Entrepreneurs with access to cheap government capital may see investing in automatic mills as a way of monopolizing profitable Food Department contracts to the exclusion of custom mills, as the government gives them preference, to protect its investment. Analysis of a series of proposals for automatic rice mills shows them all to be uneconomic in competition with custom mills without substantial subsidies.[4] This is born out in practice by the failure of the Comilla Modern Rice Mill.

Alternatives — a gradual improvement strategy

Automatic mills versus custom mills and household technology

Among the three basic technologies available, it is hard to see any justification for the import of the capital-intensive machinery and spares required for automatic mills. This is particularly true when it is considered that Bangladesh has the capacity to manufacture spares and indeed all the machinery required for custom mills. Quality is generally low but could probably be raised if the government improved the supply of raw materials on condition that quality improved, too.

Custom mills versus household milling

So far as custom mills and household milling are concerned, the farmers clearly have a large cost advantage and it seems unnecessary to increase this even further by the government provision of highly subsidized electricity. However, there are still many situations where high transport costs to the mill continue to make household husking competitive. The same strong arguments for giving preference to hand-pumps in irrigation over mechanized pumps[5] apply even more strongly to paddy husking *unless the society values female employment at a very much lower level than male employment.*

Re-organizing and improving the existing household method

An alternative strategy to the subsidized and unrestricted spread of custom mills owned by the rural rich could start by re-organizing the existing household paddy-husking labour force and, through gradual increases in investment and improvements in technology, improve their productivity and managerial capacity. IRDP and BRAC have already had considerable experience in organizing and providing loans to paddy-husking co-operatives. By simply increasing working capital to enable the group to buy and sell larger quantities at the right time, profits can be substantially increased. In addition, some small economies of scale in soaking, parboiling, and drying have been achieved. It may be possible to introduce the simple stream parboiling device used in the custom mills, and either the more productive 'Teknaf' rotary husker or smaller-scale mechanical mills might be used. This process has already been started; it should not be impossible to develop it to the point where group members can acquire and run their own mill. There is no inherent reason why all the benefits of improved technology should be at the expense of, rather than in the interests of, the existing labour force.

Conclusion

The traditional sector continues to employ a very large amount of labour despite inroads made by capital-intensive technology. However, a government strategy that encourages the import of such technology through cheap credit, subsidies or direct investment could wipe out millions of jobs very rapidly. On the other hand, a strategy combining adequate supply of raw materials, credit and organizing and managerial skills to the traditional sectors could lead to a larger utilization of under-used existing capital and labour. The two key factors are building and maintaining effective co-operative institutions at the local level and an employment-oriented set of policies at national level.

References

1. Commonwealth Associates Inc., Bangladesh Power Development Board, '1977 Rural Electrification Feasibility Study', NRFCA International Ltd., Dacca.
2. BBS, *Statistical Yearbook of Bangladesh*, Dacca, 1979.
3. Barbara Harris, *Post Harvest Rice Processing systems in Rural Bangladesh: Technology, Economics and Employment*, BRAC, Dacca, 1978.
4. Rice Processing Projects in Bangladesh: An Appraisal of a Decade of Proposals', FAO, 1978.
5. Muhammad Masum, 'Technology and Employment: A Case Study of Bangladesh', Dacca.

Further Reading

1. Mohiuddin Ahmad, 'Initiating Development', BRAC's Economic Support Programme in Sulla: Some Case Studies, BRAC, Dacca, 1978.
2. Bangladesh Handloom Board, 'Report on Bangladesh Handloom Census' 1978, Dacca.
3. BTMC, 'Report on the Operational Performance for the Month of August 1979', Dacca.
4. Nuimuddin Chowdhury, 'Resource Allocation in Handloom Industries in Three Areas of Bangladesh: Some Findings', BIDS, Dacca.
5. Rizwanul Islam, 'Some Constraints in the Choice of Technology', The Bangladesh Development Studies, Vol. V. No. 3, BIDS, Dacca.
6. Planning Commission, 'The First Five Year Plan 1973-8', Dacca, 1973.
7. 'The Two Year Plan 1978-80', Dacca, 1978.
8. Frances Stewart and Paul Streeten, 'Conflicts between Output and Employment Objectives in Developing Countries', The Bangladesh Economic Review, Vol. 1, No. 1, BIDS, Dacca.

A HULLER FOR PRODUCING UNPOLISHED RICE

Willard Unruh

Rice is probably eaten by more people than any other cereal, but in order to prepare it the outer husk must first be removed and this is a troublesome task. For centuries, hulling has been done by some kind of mortar and pestle arrangement, but because this method is so slow and laborious, power-driven hullers have proved popular. Aside from large commercial mills, in this part of Asia the steel roll huller is very popular. Low price is its only advantage. The disadvantages are high power consumption, a high rate of breakage, and the grinding of the bran and a significant amount of rice into the hull, making it fit only for cattle

Huller in use

Frame and iron parts

feed; and not very good feed at that, as the hull contains silica from which cattle, in time, get silicosis. Because of the wastage, India is seeking to outlaw the steel roll huller.

The cone-type hand-operated huller described here has been developed by the UMN (United Mission to Nepal). It produces a superior-head rice and is easy enough for children to operate.

The importance of unpolished rice

Little attention has been drawn to the great nutritional losses in polished rice because it has been considered impossible to change people's food habits. Many people suffering simple vitamin B deficiencies have come to UMN health clinics, especially in the Kathmandu valley surrounding the capital city, where steel roll hullers have been introduced. Amazingly, these people make marked improvement within two weeks, not from vitamins or medicine, but by adding one tablespoon of rice polishings to their food daily. For this reason, and because many areas of Nepal still do not have any sort of power huller, UMN nutritionists strongly urged that we develop a simple huller to produce unpolished rice.

Table 1 compares yields of three methods of hulling, also showing that in hand hulling the percentage of hulled and broken grains vary with the rate of feed. Although the actual quantity of vitamins and minerals in rice is not very high, because such large amounts are eaten, the losses from polishing and breakage become significant, as shown in Table 2.

18

Table 1.

Hulling method	Rate	Variety	Mois-ture	Sample Wt.	Paddy on %	Net	Hull on %	Mill yield	Head yield	Broken	Germ % in head
Steel roll	200 Kg/hr	IR 24	7%	8.478% Kg	42g 0.5%	8.436 Kg	2.642 31.3%	5.794 68.7%	4.595 54.5%	1.199 14.2%	2%
Foot-operated mortar, pestle	6 Kg/hr	Man-suli	10.4%	885g	6.3 0.1%	878.7	300.9 33.5%	597.5 66.5%	367.9 41%	227.6 25.3%	11%
Foot-operated mortar, pestle	6 Kg/hr	IR 24	8.8%	1 Kg	40.4 4%	959.6	270 28.1%	698.5 71.9%	373.7 38.9%	315.1 32.9%	28%
Hand huller	6 Kg/hr	Man-suli	7%	500g	82.5 16.5%	417.5	87.5 21%	330 79%	320.1 76.7%	9.9 2.4%	98%
Hand huller	4 Kg/hr	IR 24	7%	500g	4.8 1%	495.2	115.5 23.3%	379.7 76.7%	352.2 71.9%	23.5 4.7%	98%
Hand huller	3.8 Kg/hr	IR 24	8.8%	500g	4.5 0.9%	495.5	109.3 22%	386.3 785	344.8 69.6%	41.4 8.4%	90%

Note: Mill yield is the total amount of rice from hulling including brokens.
Head yield is whole grains including three-quarters or more of the kernel.

Table 2.

| | COMPOSITION PER 100g RAW | | | | | QUANTITY AND % OF DAILY REQUIREMENT | | | | |
	Hand pounded	Milled	Activity	Daily Req.	Rice eaten daily	Hand pounded		Milled		
Thiamine B1	0.21 mg	0.06 mg	Adoles-	2 mg		0.945	47.3%	0.27	13.5%	
Riboflavin B2	0.16	0.06	cent boy	2.2	450 g	0.72	32.7%	0.27	12.3%	
Niacin B3	3.9	1.9	Man: heavy	26		17.55	67.5%	8.55	32.9%	
Protein	7.5 g	6.8 g	work	55 g		33.75	61.4%	30.6	55.6%	
Thiamine B1	0.21 mg	0.06 mg	Woman:	1.25		0.735	58.8%	0.21	16.8%	
Riboflavin B2	0.16	0.06	average	1.35	350 g	0.56	41.5%	0.21	15.6%	
Niacin B3	3.9	1.9	activity	16.5		13.65	82.7%	6.65	40%	
Protein	7.5 g	6.8 g		45 g		26.25	58.3%	23.8	52.9%	
Thiamine B1	0.21 mg	0.06 mg		0.6 mg		0.315	52.5%	0.09	15%	
Riboflavin B2	0.16	0.06	Child	0.7	150 g	0.24	34.3%	0.09	12.9%	
Niacin B3	3.9	1.9		8		5.85	73%	2.85	35.6%	
Protein	7.5 g	6.8 g		29 g		11.25	38.8%	10.2	35.2%	

Miriam Krantz, UMN Nutritionist, had this to say about protein content. 'Although the difference between hand-pounded and milled rice does not seem very great, it is significant because it is the protein contained in the germ of the kernel which has a high biological value, not that in the endosperm (tissue around the embryo). The amino acid, lysine, is especially low in this part but is remarkably high in the germ. Cereals are in general low in lysine. But unpolished rice has a higher content of this amino acid than most cereals. If even one essential amino acid is partially missing . . . the result is that *all* amino acids are reduced in the same proportion.'

Ms Krantz continues: 'In other words the amount of protein in the food (as shown in the tables) is not the amount of protein that the body can fully use unless it has a high biological value. So without the germ of the rice kernel the percentage of the rest of the protein that the body can absorb is greatly reduced, even when eaten along with pulses. In the case of rice the amino acids, lysine and threonine, are the limiting ones.'

It can be argued that it is impossible to change people's eating habits toward unpolished rice, especially as the cooking procedure is a little different. However, when healthful food is in short supply it seems reasonable to make the effort.

Constructing the huller

The hand huller looks like the traditional stone grain grinder, which helps to make it acceptable. The mating surfaces, instead of being flat, slope to the centre at a 15° angle, enabling the paddy to move through smoothly. The bottom part, or the body, is made first. The iron frame is sunk into the ground which is sloped so it becomes the form for the underside of the body. Concrete is poured on to the form and tamped down to produce a smooth surface.

Several days later the top or cone is cast inside the body so that the surfaces will match perfectly. Newspaper or a thin film of mud prevents the two parts from sticking together. The cone is 3cm smaller in diameter than the inside of the body and its edge is formed by a sheet metal strip 1cm wide. The top of the cone is sloped about 15°. The concrete must be kept moist throughout the curing process.

After curing for about a week the cone is rotated inside the body to check for possible high spots which should be worked down. Tapering the outside lower edge of the cone helps prevent paddy from being ejected. The sloped surface in the body is covered with two layers of truck inner tube. Half sections should be cut from the sides of the tube while the part which sits against the rim is discarded. Ordinary glue holds the lower layer to the concrete while rubber cement is used for the second.

Use of the huller

The feeding rate of the paddy influences the percentage hulled. Women familiar with the stone mill tend to feed too slowly at first, but a little experimentation will determine the optimum rate. Paddy should be as dry as possible to make hulling easier and to minimize breakage.

The cost of producing hullers in quantity is about US$6 for steel legs and under $5 for concrete legs, with cement costing $5 per bag. As to durability, one unit shows barely-perceptible wear after hulling 60kg. The rubber should last one family for several years.

SUCCESSFULLY PROCESSING SORGHUM

Garry Whitby

It is all too rarely that one can report a success story of the magnitude of the IDRC/RIIC sorghum dehuller programme. Even rarer to report its continuing success which is spreading through Africa: to Tanzania, and, more surprisingly, to South Africa. The story began in 1975 when the Government of Botswana asked the Botswana Agricultural Marketing Board (BAMB) to investigate the mechanical processing of sorghum to remove the back-breaking, time-consuming toil of many women who spend hours pounding away at the sorghum grain.

In co-operating with the International Development Research Centre (IDRC), BAMB installed Botswana's first commercial sorghum mill at Pitsane in 1977, and this was working completely under local management producing *Bopi Jwa Mabele* by late 1978. By making processed sorghum available, the mill regenerated a demand for Botswana's traditional food, which the imported mealie meal (maize), had been replacing. Clearly, even at a cost greater than the mealie meal, the people of Botswana preferred sorghum or *mabele* as they call it. The commercial mill was large, however, capable of processing four to five tonnes per day, and it relied on large supplies of sorghum from BAMB, and on a road and rail network, in order to operate efficiently. Realizing this, and supported by reports on consumer preferences,[1] the Rural Industries Innovation Centre (RIIC), in further collaboration with IDRC, set about designing a smaller and more versatile unit for the varying needs of rural communities who grew their own sorghum. Between 1978 and 1980 RIIC redesigned, developed, and tested various prototypes of a scaled-down dehuller. The eventual outcome was a machine, smaller than the Pitsane model, which could operate at high speeds, and process (ironically) the same sort of quantities. In 1979, the RIIC installed one of their models in their home village of Kanye and later that year another at Pelegano Village Industries in Gabane for trials. A survey in Kanye[2] clearly showed the need for such machines, as did later reports on the sorghum mills placed in Moshupar, Mahalapye, Tlokweng and Gabane.[3]

The sorghum mill at Kanye is saving many women and children hours of back-breaking pounding every day. (Photo: Michael Kahn/Photopics Ltd.)

A seminar was held in September 1979 for potential investors in the equipment with RIIC taking orders. They produced a mill owners' handbook[4] and a promotional booklet[5] clearly describing the benefits of an investment in the equipment with information on how to run a business as a mill owner. The first course for mill owners took place in February 1980 and production of three dehullers began early that year, followed by eight more later in 1980. Sales to date total thirty-six units with firm orders for eleven more.

Support services
With such a rapid development and uptake of a technology it is not surprising that there were a few problems with the early machines. A Post-Harvest Technology Programme[6] was set up by RIIC's parent company, Rural Industries Promotion (RIP) to investigate claims and counter-claims of incorrect user practices and low quality manufacture. The outcome was a need for technical refinements, a need for educational and organizational support for the mill owners, and a need for an infrastructure to provide quick and effective support (such as the supply of spares, repair and maintenance). Perhaps more important, however, was

the establishment of the Botswana Mill Owners' Association in 1983, for the owners to share a forum of mutual interest.

The RIIC design lends itself to batch service milling as well as continuous commercial milling. The RIIC handbook recommends the combination of service milling in the morning and commerical milling in the afternoon. Thus villagers can either buy sorghum meal or bring their own grain for milling.

An end to pounding

Service milling for women means relief from a laborious daily task. The traditional method of milling the sorghum involves soaking the grain in water for half-an-hour to an hour to soften it, as this helps to remove the bran. It is then put into a wooden mortar, and pounded with a pestle until the bran is separated, with winnowing from time to time to remove the bran. When enough bran is removed, the dehulled grain is pounded further into pulverized meal. Four kilograms of sorghum are required to feed a family of six for about two days — at least three hours of hard work.[1]

A survey[7] in 1981 concluded that the mill could release up to four hours per day of a woman's and her children's time. It indicated that this was usefully spent in 'productive' activities such as mixing clay, weeding, knitting or beer brewing; and in the case of children it was spent studying and reading!

Commercial milling on the other hand has meant a reduction in the country's dependence on imported food, and has enabled the consumers to obtain their preferred food. This has meant, however, that mill owners wishing to secure local supplies for commercial milling have had to increase the producer price for sorghum grain. In 1982, sorghum prices were higher than import prices and this meant a need for import bans to avoid profits going across the border to South Africa. In 1985 the government put a levy on sorghum prices to encourage the sale and purchase of sorghum from BAMB. It is such policies that the Botswana Mill Owners Association discuss, to protect their interest.

The complete mill comprises a dehuller, to remove the bran; and a hammer mill to grind the dehulled grain into meal. Currently the system costs about P12,500 (£6,250) of which P5,500 (£2,250) is the diesel engine. Finance is available from the National Development Bank, the Botswana Government's Financial Assistance Policy and other sources. The thirty-six mills sold so far are run by co-operatives, brigade centres and private individuals providing over 250 direct jobs, as well as the numerous benefits already mentioned.[8]

How it works

The traditional method of milling sorghum begins with soaking the grain to soften it and make the bran easier to remove. When enough soaking time has passed, a portion of wet grain is put in a stamping block or on grinding stones. By continuously moving the grinding stone or stamping the pestle in the mortar across the wet grain, the bran is removed. The grain is winnowed occasionally to remove the bran from the sorghum kernels. This is repeated until an acceptable amount of bran has been removed. The dehulled grain is then ground into meal by further stamping or grinding.

The mechanical processing of sorghum follows the same basic principle of separating the bran from the grain. The main difference is that the grain is not soaked before starting. Soaking the grain decreases the length of time the meal will last before it goes bad. Removing the bran in the mechanical method is done by stirring and shaking the grain at a very high speed.

The key element of the milling system is the dehuller. Abrasive discs or stones set on a horizontal shaft rotate at high speed inside the casing. The hulls are 'rubbed' off by the grinding action of the whirling stones and the friction of other grains. When grain first enters the dehuller casing it is retained for a brief period before the exit chute is opened. The rate of flow of the grain is adjusted so that the grain is kept in the casing just long enough to remove the desired amount of bran.

The dehuller can be made in developing countries, using readily available — or cheaply imported — materials, and local resources. The stones in the Kanye and Pitsane dehullers are simple carborundum grinding wheels, the kind made for sharpening tools.

The bran is then taken away from the dehulled grain by a fan that uses moving air in much the same way as hand winnowing. The bran is collected and used for brewing beer or for animal feed, and the dehulled grain is moved to the hammer mill. Here it is ground into meal. The mechanical method is known as 'dry abrasion' because water is not added to the grain at any stage of processing.

Why it works

The credit for this success story is due to the Rural Industries Innovation Centre, for maintaining the momentum of interest through many changes of personnel over the period of the project.

Many other institutions suffer from personnel changes every two or three years, and a general lack of interest among new recruits to take over where someone else left off. In this example, however, it was clear that the technology was well researched from the basic need, through consumer preference, technology choice, and carefully monitored implementation, to the impact of the technology on the people it was designed to help — and who could ignore that! The confidence of RIIC that they had got the right technology was highlighted in the setting up of the Post Harvest Technology Programme, and their continued interest in the technology has been demonstrated by the establishment of the Botswana Mill Owners Association.

An approach from South Africa regarding an export order for P300,000 must surely say it all.

References

1. Eisener, N., and MacFarlane, C., 'Overview of the sorghum milling pilot project — Botswana', IDRC, Canada, October 1978.
2. Sekelenyane, J., 'Sorghum mill survey — Kanye', RIIC, Botswana, August 1979.
3. Norahan-Parker, D., 'The impact of sorghum mills on four rural communities in Botswana', March 1982.
4. *Lelewala (lele tlhobolang bukana ya Motsameisi*, RIIC, Botswana, 1979.
5. Eisener, N., *Tlhobololo le tshilo ya mabele*, RIIC, Botswana, 1979.
6. 'Post-Harvest Technology Programme — Final Report', RIP, Botswana, March 1984.
7. Haride, J., *Sorghum milling in Botswana — A Development Impact Case Study*, IDRC, Canada, January 1982.
8. Inger, D., 'Poverty and "development" in Botswana and the potential for rural non-agricultural production', RIP, Botswana, January 1985.

STORING GRAIN ON THE FARM
Robin Boxall

The five cereal grains which dominate agriculture in tropical and subtropical regions are rice, maize, sorghum, millet and wheat. In some areas pulse grains or root crops predominate as the major food source. The local importance of specific crops is dictated by geographical and climatic patterns, traditional preferences and opportunities for marketing surpluses.

In those countries where farming is predominantly at the subsistence level, it is estimated that between 60 per cent and 70 per cent of cereal grain productionis retained at the farm level. The farmer must conserve his staple food to feed his dependants and livestock from one harvest to the next. If he produces a surplus and wishes to take advantage of seasonal rises in prices, he must be able to conserve his grain for long periods without spoilage or loss.

A striking feature of traditional post-harvest systems is the manner in which they have so clearly evolved to suit local customs and social and economic conditions and have become associated with local varieties of grain. Over several generations, farmers' capability has become finely adapted in two ways: through the development of their skills in harvesting, threshing, drying, storing and processing, as well as by their careful selection of those grain varieties best suited to particular needs. The traditional farming practices, especially the storage methods, are often considered inefficient and wasteful when compared to larger mechanized farms. Serious losses have been attributed to the traditional farm sector but it has been clearly shown that the losses are often quite low, especially when related to the cost of farmers' efforts required for further loss reduction.

Causes of loss in stores

There are a formidable number of factors with which farmers must contend if they are to conserve their mature crop without spoilage and loss. These are considered below in sequence. Loss and deterioration of grain during storage may occur because:
○ The condition of the grain received into store is unsatisfactory.
○ The store itself is unsatisfactory.

Woven basket type of grain store for maize used in Zambia

○ The management of the store is inadequate and unfavourable
   conditions are allowed to develop.

Good storage must begin with cereals and legumes entering the
store in good condition, but deterioration of the grains can begin
even before harvest or during the stages of harvesting, threshing,
drying or transportation of grain to store. In the tropics grain
crops are likely to be infested in the field by storage insects which
fly out from nearby stores. These insects develop within grains
and so after harvest they are carried as hidden infestation into
store where they will later emerge if conditions are favourable.
Fungi and bacteria may attack grains especially in wet harvesting
conditions and rodents and birds may attack the standing crop
leaving damaged grains which are more suceptible to attack by
insects and micro-organisms in store.

The timing of harvesting has a significant effect on subsequent
deterioration of grain. Premature harvesting will result in a large
proportion of immature grains that, because of high moisture
content, will deteriorate rapidly in store. On the other hand, if
harvesting is delayed too long then the mature grains may be
attacked in the field by insects, micro-organisms and animal pests
and may be physically damaged by cracking as a result of
repeated wetting and drying, for example, by rain or dew followed
by hot sun.

Frequently it is necessary to dry grain to a safe moisture content
for storage, that is, one which inhibits growth of micro-organisms

or limits the development of insects. Care must be taken to avoid rapid drying or over-drying which may result in cracked grains leading to more rapid deterioration in storage. The grain itself may have properties unsuitable for longer-term storage through deficiencies in the seed coat or the endosperm.

Deterioration during storage caused by the principal agents, micro-organisms, insects and vertebrate pests is influenced by the storage design and storage environment. A fram grain store should be structurally sound and waterproof; but this is not sufficient to prevent deterioration. Growth of micro-organisms occurs when grain is exposed to high humidities and the seriousness of insect infestation tends to increase at higher temperatures and tropical temperatures are typically conducive to maximum reproduction. A well-designed store will therefore include features that afford maximum protection against the more obvious forms of deterioration caused by rain and ground moisture, limit high humidities and high temperatures and provide a barrier to insect and rodent attack.

When the requirements for such a safe storage have been fulfilled, deterioration may still occur if the store is poorly managed. Reservoirs of insect infestation will persist if grain residues build up through poor standards of store hygiene, or if infested produce remains in store from one season to the next.

Traditional storage methods

Traditional grain storage systems have evolved over generations to satisfy the requirements for safe storage within the limits of the local culture, and throughout the developing world a great variety of storage containers can be found. Although the basic concepts may be similar, the appearance and methods of construction of the store may vary considerably according to local custom. Generally the containers are made from plant material, mud or stone, often raised on platforms and provided with a thatched roof. Small quantities of seed grain may be kept inside the farmer's house stored in containers such as baskets, clay pots and gourds although the use of sacks and small oil drums is also quite widespread.

The type of grain store is often determined by the local cropping patterns. For example, in areas where two or more crops per year can be grown, the farmer requires only a relatively temporary store capable of holding sufficient grain to last until the next harvest. However, in areas where rainfall is unpredictable and crop failures may be common there is an obvious need to provide

A farmer holds in his left hand an ear of maize which is covered by the sheathing leaves, and in his right hand a poorly covered ear typical of many high-yielding varieties

more permanent facilities for long-term storage.

Drying is a vital pre-storage stage, especially in humid areas, since moisture may be the most important factor determining whether and to what extent grain will be liable to deterioration during storage. Often a special structure is needed to allow drying of the crop whilst affording some protection. In southern Ghana, for example, where the humidity is high immediately after harvest, a raised circular platform on which unsheathed maize cobs, supported by a girdle of grass ropes, encloses an inner, loosely filled area, and the whole structure is provided with a thatched roof for protection.

In other parts of Africa dual purpose drying and storage structures called 'cribs' are found. In east Africa they consist of containers made of wood or bamboo with definite walls, a floor and a roof. The walls are open weave to allow free movement of air throughout the structure.

With the exception of sealed containers (such as, underground pit stores and some small pots, gourds), the traditional structures provide little protection against insect and rodent attack, particularly where the climate is warm and humid or where grain is stored for long periods. Under these conditions losses do occur, but a number of long-term studies have clearly shown that storage losses are much lower than previously reported. In general the traditional methods of storage work well, containing losses at about the five per cent level, as long as they are in balance with the rest of the farming system. (See Table 1.)

A close examination of the traditional farming system reveals that, not surprisingly, crop varieties have often been selected by the farmer for their ability to resist pest attack during storage. Traditional methods of insect control are employed, often extremely successfully, to reduce the amount of damage caused to the grain to an acceptable level. Commonly used traditional methods of insect control include the mixing of sand or wood ash to provide a physical barrier to pests, and the use of aromatic plant materials as repellants. It is important to realize that such traditional insect control techniques are usually specific to a

Table 1. Examples of reliable estimates of post-harvest grain losses storage at farm level

Country	Crop	Period of storage (months)	Cause of loss	Estimated % loss of weight and range
Zambia[1]	maize	7	insects	1.7 to 5.6
India[3]	paddy	7	insects, rodents, mould	4.26 ± 1.33
Kenya[5]	maize	up to 9	insects, rodents	3.53 ± 0.25
Malawi[7]	maize	up to 9	insects	3.2 ± 3.4 1.8 ± 3.5
	sorghum	up to 9	insects	1.7 ± 0.5
Nepal[2]	maize	6	insects, rodents	5.7 ± 3.2
	wheat	3	mould	2.4 ± 1.9
	paddy	8	insects	3.4 ± 2.2
Swaziland[6]	maize	unspecified	insects mould rodents	3.66 0.53 0.16
Bangladesh*	raw and parvoiled paddy	3-4	insects rodents	2.4 (rice equivalent) (average for 3 crop seasons)
Honduras[4]	maize	7	insects	5.5

Storage methods for cobs of maize in southern Ghana

particular region or community and that attempts to introduce from elsewhere have largely been unsuccessful, either because the practice has been unacceptable socially, or the technique failed to give adequate protection under local conditions.

The need for improved storage

Considerable effort is being devoted to increasing the production of food grains particularly in developing countries and as a result new cereal and legume varieties have been developed which show substantial increases in yields over the traditional varieties. The changes consequent upon the introduction of improved crop production programmes which include the adoption of new high-yielding varieties and multiple cropping techniques disturb the traditional capability to conserve grain and increase the risk of loss. Not only has the increase in production placed a strain on the farm-level storage capacity, it has resulted in a number of serious post-harvest problems, especially for the small farmer.

Some of the new high-yielding varieties can be grown outside the normal growing season and while this allows two or sometimes three crops per year, an unfortunate consequence is that the farmer sometimes has to harvest in the pouring rain instead of during a cool dry period. His traditional resources and experience are not able to cope adequately with the problems of having to dry, thresh and store grain under adverse weather conditions.

The qualities of traditional grain varieties (namely hard endosperm and good husk cover in maize) help to protect the grain from insect attack but the high-yielding varieties, although possessing improved nutritional value, unfortunately have introduced some characteristics which render them more vulnerable to spoilage. Often the grains are softer and extremely susceptible to insect attack.

The improvement of storage structures as a means of reducing loss has been the subject of attention in many tropical countries. Sometimes it is possible to introduce relatively simple adaptations to traditional structures. In Malawi for example, the traditional storage container for maize is a cylindrical crib constructed from woven sticks. In areas with prolonged rains it has been found that maize does not dry adequately before the onset of the rainy season, and goes mouldy. In one attempt to solve this problem a modified design in the shape of a rectangular crib developed at the African Rural Storage Centre, Nigeria, was shown to be promising experimentally. Unfortunately, the farmers have shown some reluctance to adopt this new but technically sound design, and so the problem has been overcome by simple modifications to the existing structure. It is recommended that the diameter should not exceed 1.8m and that mud should be applied to the external walls just before the onset of the rains. These two measures enable grain to dry to a satisfactory level and the plastering restricts the amount of moisture taken up by the cobs so they remain free from mould.

The use of grain driers has been considered for farm-level drying in several countries but experience has shown that the use of small-scale driers is not a suitable answer to drying needs. Moreover the fuel supply from firewood or fossil fuels makes the method both economically and environmentally less attractive than free ventilation methods.

New designs

New designs of storage structures have been introduced successfully in many countries, especially where farmers have shown a willingness to adopt new farming techniques. In India and parts of Central and South America, metal grain bins are finding wide acceptance. However, the successful adoption of

Metal grain storage tanks covered with thatch, typical of those found in Botswana and Swaziland

such containers is dependent upon changes in storage management practices. For example, more attention must be paid to how to dry the grain if the problems of mould damage are to be avoided when storing in the metal bin. Elsewhere, improved grain bins have not met with the same success; for example in Ghana and Zambia concrete stoves were developed, and although shown to be structurally sound and technically effective, farmers found them to be unacceptable for many reasons, which included rising costs, shortage of materials and difficulties associated with construction.

Even with the improvement of storage structures, there is still a need for reliable and effective methods of pest prevention and control during the storage period. Since the traditional ashes and dusts seem unable to provide a satisfactory level of protection to the hybrid varieties of grain the farmer could turn to the highly effective and safe insecticides which have shown promise in experimental studies, but in practice serious drawbacks arise. There are problems such as formulation and stability of suitably dilute dusts to be overcome, and there are marketing and distribution difficulties, particularly in developing countries. On top of this there are now proven cases where resistance to certain pesticides renders their use ineffective against grain pests. Plant breeders who can successfully combine a high-yielding variety with improved storage characteristics, will have made significant long-term progress.

The need for caution

The total farming system in its primitive form seems less hazardous than when it has been only partly altered. Improvements have often been introduced into subsistence farming systems without taking account of the delicate balance which has been achieved between agricultural and natural forces, and consequently, new problems have been created. To some extent this is because of the introduction of hybrid varieties, where, though yields are undoubtedly higher, so also are the losses in store through insect and fungal attack.

The introduction of change in agriculture requires a thorough understanding of the problems it will cause, sound technical advice to meet them and an effective training and extension programme for implementation. If changes are to be introduced with maximum benefit they must be available when and where required and at an affordable cost to the farmer. These requirements have rarely been met effectively in the case of insecticides.

There are still many aspects of farmer storage needing more study and research to establish the optimum methods of storage appropriate to the farming system. Trained and mobile extension staff can, however, make a significant improvement to small-scale storage by the application of known and established techniques.

References

1. Adams, J.M., Harman, G.W., 'The evaluation of losses in maize stored on a selection of small farms in Zambia with particular reference to the development of methodology', Report G.109, Tropical Products Institute, London, 1977.
2. Boxall, R.A., Gillett, R., 'Farmer level storage losses in Eastern Nepal', Report G.157. Tropical Products Institute, London, 1982.
3. Boxall, R.A., Greeley, M., Tyagi, D.S. with Lipton, M. and Neelakanta, J., 'The prevention of farm level food grain storage losses in India: a social cost-benefit analysis', IDS Research Report, Institute of Development Studies, University of Sussex, Brighton, 1978.
4. de Breve, M., Raboud, G., Sieber, J., Perdomo, J.A. and Velasquez, J.E., 'Proyecto Post-Cosecha: informe sobre los primeros resultados', Ministerio de Recursos Naturales and Cooperación Suiza al Desarrollo, Tegucigalpa, Honduras, 1982.
5. de Lima, C.P.F., 'The assessment of losses due to insects and rodents in maize stored for subsistence in Kenya', Tropical Stored Products Information, 38, 1979.

6. de Lima, C.P.F., 'Strengthening of the Food Conservation and Crop Storage Section', Ministry of Agriculture and Cooperatives, Project SWA/002/PFL Final Report, FAO, Rome, 1982.

7. Golob, P., 'A practical assessment of food losses sustained during storage by smallholder farmers in the Shire Valley Agricultural Development Project area of Malawi', 1978-9, Report G.154, Tropical Products Institute, London, 1981.

COTTAGE INDUSTRIES FOR PRODUCING WEANING FOODS
Gill Gordon

Growth slows down in many children between the ages of six months and three years and 30 per cent or more may be underweight for their age. The weaning period is a risky time because children must learn to eat new foods and cope with new pathogens. Many children eat too few calories and too little protein, vitamins and minerals for their needs over this period.

Special weaning foods are needed because children are at risk of malnutrition during the weaning period.

One problem is that children are fed a very watery cereal gruel with no protein- or energy-rich ingredients. They would have to drink four litres of this a day to meet their complete energy and growth needs. Another problem is that adult meals are unsuitable for young children because they contain hot spices, hard or fibrous pieces, or are simply too thick. Their protein to energy ratio and energy density is also too low.

Yet another problem for children during the weaning period is that meals are only prepared once or twice a day because of time constraints and fuel shortage. The problem worsens in the farming season. Young children are either given breast-milk only throughout the day, or they are given meals which have been kept in the heat for many hours. In the warm rainy season, diarrhoea pathogens in meals rise to dangerous levels after just a few hours.

Disappointing results

Nutritional workers spend considerable time teaching mothers how to prepare special weaning mixes for their children. These are usually 'multimixes' made from a mixture of local cereals, legumes and oil-seeds. Mothers are asked to prepare fresh foods for each meal and to feed the children frequently through the day. The results of these programmes have frequently been disappointing.

○ In Ghana, mothers reported that they were unable to prepare the weaning food because they were too busy farming and trading. They were willing to buy ready-made fish powder from the child welfare clinic to add to the gruel.[1]

Growing slows in many children between six months and three years of age

○ Nurses in Tanzania accompaniedmothers about their tasks for two days. They returned exhausted and reported that if they were these mothers they would never manage to find time to make special weaning foods.[2]

○ In Ife, Nigeria, mothers relied on ready-to-eat purchased meals at midday and did not have time to prepare special meals for children.

Mothers in Africa buy expensive commercial baby foods primarily for their convenience, palatability and safety rather than status. In west Africa, mothers tend to spend their independent income on a meal for their children at noon.[3]

There appears to be great potential for the creation and expansion of home or cottage industries to produce weaning foods, or for vendors of ready-to-eat meals and snacks to add a baby food to their usual products. This home industry would have several advantages over large-scale weaning food industries:

○ The processed foods or meals would be available on the doorstep of the consumers, at times and at prices which suited them.

○ Small-scale women producers could control aflatoxin contamination by selecting fresh local ground-nuts and limiting storage time. The problems with controlling aflatoxin levels is a major barrier to large-scale production, and this contributed to the failure of three weaning food enterprises in west Africa.[4]

○ The women would get immediate feedback on the acceptance of their product and could adapt it to match the demand, as well as the availability of ingredients at different times of year.

○ Women would greatly benefit from the income.

We can learn from the experiences of women's groups around the world to see how weaning food industries could best be organized.

Food vendors in Nigeria

A home economist from Ife University taught food vendors how to make soft pepper-free bean and ground-nut meals for weaning children.[5] After a few weeks the vendors stopped selling the meals because the price of ingredients rose sharply. Then four women agreed to make half-sized loaves of cold *eko* (made by steaming maize flour) containing dried fish and palm oil at the regular price. The product had these advantages:

○ The ingredients are available locally and prices were stable.

○ The method required little extra labour.

○ *Eko* is not prepared with pepper.

○ The packaging was inexpensive and hygienic.

○ Sales of regular *eko* were maintained.

○ Vendors could afford the initial cost of ingredients.

Everyone approved of the *eko omode* for a few days and then production stopped. This was because vendors can sell the unimproved type of *eko* for up to 24 hours after packaging, but the new recipe for *eko omode* spoilt within six hours. Often the women could not sell the food quickly enough, which wasted time and money.

Then one vendor was given credit, to cope with the fluctuating prices of beans and ground-nuts. She prepared the baby foods irregularly because she doubted if they would prove profitable. The programme then hired a labourer to cook and sell the baby foods. Accounts were kept of income and expenditure and this

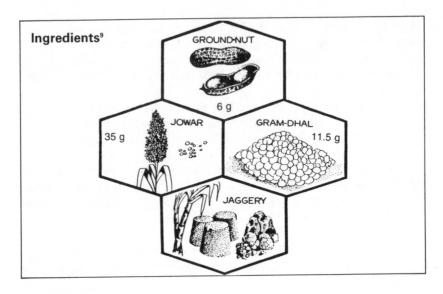

Ingredients[9]

GROUND-NUT

6 g

JOWAR

35 g

GRAM-DHAL

11.5 g

JAGGERY

showed the women that they could make small but steady profits on baby foods.

Several women offered to sell the baby food as a sideline to their usual wares. The profit from the first venture was used as a loan for another woman to start a baby food business. She in turn repaid the loan after the harvest, and another vendor was helped to start her business with it. The labourer moved on to another village where another vendor benefited from her profits. This financial contribution was an important incentive for food vendors to experiment with a new industry.

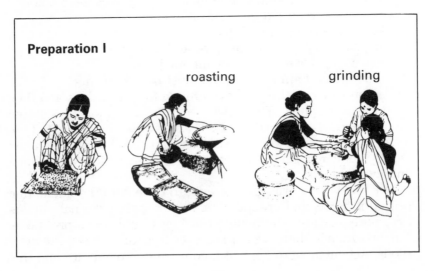

Preparation I

roasting

grinding

Preparation II

mixing

bagging

Women's groups in Ghana and India

In Ghana, UNICEF is assisting women's groups in rural areas to buy grinding mills, and to use them to produce an instant weaning food both for sale and their own use. The cheapest available cereals — beans and oil-seeds — are roasted separately and ground twice into a fine flour or paste. Four measures of cereal are mixed with one measure of beans. The flour is kept in a tightly closed container or sealed in plastic bags for sale. It should not be stored for more than twoweeks.

In Hyderabad, women's groups produce an instant weaning food called 'the Hyderabad mix'. The mixture contains at least one legume and one cereal so that the amino acid balance is satisfactory. The mix contains ground-nuts and local sugar, both of which provide a concentrated source of energy. This is essential so young children with small stomachs can obtain their calorie needs from the volume of food that they can eat. The ingredients vary with seasonal availability.

The grains are cleaned by hand, dry roasted over a fire and ground on a stone. The flours are mixed, put into plastic bags, checked for weight and sealed using candle wax. The packets are sold on the market or distributed through nursery schools. Each packet provides about 250 calories, 10 grams of protein and 50 i.u. of vitamin A. Literally thousands of children have benefited from these packets, and the women's groups make a profit. Children (and adults!) eat the plain powder, or make it into a porridge with water or milk, or cook it as chapatis, or roll it into sweet jaggery balls.

The foods can be made all over Africa as they need only cereals, legumes, oil-seeds and flour

A similar weaning mix was produced by a home science college near Madras.[7] The product was demonstrated to women's groups in villages around Tamil Nadu, and one group decided to go into production on a commercial basis. The Social Service Association of the home science college gave a loan of Rs.1,000 to set up the production unit and obtained the necessary licence for the group. Various agencies helped to market the food mix.

Testing the market

A demonstration and sales campaign was conducted at the co-operative supermarket in Coimbatore to test the market response. The product was exhibited at a World Vegetarian Congress in Madras and in stalls at trade fairs in the neighbourhood. People liked the product because it was cheap, tasty and of good quality. The patent from the well-known home science college made it acceptable and caught people's attention.

Paediatricians were asked to endorse the product for feeding malnourished children. Nursery and boarding schools were approached, soon several orphanages and schools began ordering regular supplies of the food mix. This gave financial security to the women's group processing the mix.

Making biscuits

Bakers could easily add high-energy and high-protein biscuits to their range of products.[8] Biscuits contain little water so are very high in calories. They have a long, safe storage life and are very popular with children. They can be made from any types of locally available cereals, legumes, oil-seeds and oil mixed with a little wheat flour.

Two biscuits made using the recipe shown will give a child the same amount of nutrition as two large pieces of meat, and the same amount of energy as two cupfuls of *akasa*.

Women could make these biscuits for the market, day-care centres and schools using a clay bread oven or a five-gallon oil drum over a coal put with a layer of sand and charcoal at the top.

It is important to remember the following points:
○ Make the weaning food from a mixture of ingredients, including a cereal, a legume, an oil-seed (or groundnuts), a fat or oil and if possible a source of vitamin A such as red palm oil.
○ Use only ingredients that you know to be fresh and free from mould.
○ Add as little water as possible to the mixture to increase energy content.
○ Test the product for acceptability. You could do this by asking tasters to put different colour beans in a tin for 'like', 'not sure' and 'don't like'.

People should only prepare a small quantity of the mix at a time for small children, so that it is not kept for long. This is especially important if it is an instant food mixed with unboiled water. People wanting to sell their product should be on the look-out for markets in schools and health services, as well as local mothers, to achieve a steady demand.

Health workers, women's organizations, credit unions and appropriate technology groups could work together to assist women to increase their income and improve the health of their children by increasing the availability of convenient, low-cost and nutritious weaning foods.

Recipe for making biscuits

○ Choose a legume, such as beans; an oil-seed such as ground-nut or sesame; and a cereal such as millet ormaize. Get some wheat flour.

○ Make sure that all the ingredients are very clean and fresh. Throw our mouldy nuts.

○ Roast the ground-nuts or sesame, taking care not to burn them. Pound and grind them into a fine flour or paste. Soak the beans, rub off the skins and dry. Grind into a fine flour.

○ Roast and grind the cereal.

○ Mix one part of the bean or sesame flour; the cereal flour; the wheat flour and the ground-nut flour. You can use any combination of flours as long as you include some wheat flour for binding, one cereal flour and one legume or oil-seed flour.

○ Add a half part of sugar. Add a teaspoonful of baking powder to each 10 big spoonfuls of the mixture.

○ Add a half part of oil or fat to mixture to increase its energy and make it crumbly. Rub it in thoroughly until you have a dryish, sand-like mixture.

○ Add water, one spoonful at a time, kneading the dough until you have a plastic but not sticky texture. Knead for five minutes until it is smooth.

○ Roll the dough out thinly (about ⅛-inch) with a corked bottle full of water. Cut into biscuits and place on a greased and floured metal sheet or tray.

○ Bake the biscuits in a fairly hot bread oven for about 15 minutes, watching to see that they do not burn. They should be quite hard.

○ Allow the biscuits to cool, and then pack them in an air-tight container.

References

1. Gordon, G., 'Implementing GOBI in the Dangbe District of Ghana — Perceptions of Mothers and Health Workers', Report to UNICEF, Accra, Ghana, 1985.
2. FAO, *Women in Food Production, Food Handling and Nutrition: with special emphasis on Africa*, Food and Nutrition Paper 8, 1979.
3. Tripp, R., *Economic strategies and nutritional status in a compound farming settlement in northern Ghana'*, doctoral dissertation, Columbia University, New York, 1978.
4. Tropical Products Institute, *'The Production of Protein Foods and Concentrates from Oil-seeds'*, G 31, 1967.
5. Lapido, P., 'Report to the Department of Home Economics', University of Ife, Nigeria, 1976.
6. Mathur, Y.C., 'Village-level Production of Supplementary Food', Indo-Dutch Project for Child Welfare, *Trop. Doctor, 6.2,* 1976.
7. Carr, M., *Blacksmith, Baker, Roofing-sheet maker: Employment for rural women in developing countries*, IT Publications, 1984.
8. Ritchie, J., *Nutrition and Families*, Macmillan, 1983.
9. Drawings taken from Morley, D., Woodland, M., *See How They Grow*, Macmillan, 1979.

THE SITUM BANANA CHIP ENTERPRISE

Rashimah New

Situm is a rural settlement about twenty kilometres out of Lae, Morobe Province. The project began about two years ago when Situm villagers started to build an addition to their shop with the intention of developing a women's food-making enterprise. They then contacted ATDI staff members and were shown how to use their surplus bananas to make deep-fried chips and to seal them hygienically in plastic bags for sale to the public. The project has been strongly supported by the village people who have enthusiastically carried out the major portion of the groundwork.

The product, under the brand name, 'Mr Banana Sip', consists of lengthwise sliced, deep fried and salted banana chips, similar in taste, appearance and texture to potato chips. The chips are sealed in polyethylene bags with an enclosed printed label stating

Peeling and slicing the bananas

45

GOSHEN COLLEGE LIBRARY
GOSHEN, INDIANA

Frying the slices in hot oil on the Lorena stove

the name, minimum weight of 35g, and name and address of the producer. They are sold commercially through retail stores in Lae.

Selection of bananas

Any type of banana can be used for the production of banana chips. The bananas must be harvested and processed in the mature green stage, before they turn yellow. Immature green bananas give chips which are less satisfactory in colour, texture and taste. Ripe bananas are not suitable because they are difficult to slice, take longer to dry and do not retain their crispness.

For the Situm project the variety known as Yava was chosen because:
○ It is the most readily obtainable, being available all the year round.
○ It is easy to peel and less liable to change colour when cut. (Some varieties of banana turn brown very quickly when exposed to the air.)
○ It is the cheapest.

Yava is a very common variety, resistant to leaf spot disease, able to withstand drought, and tolerant of shade. It grows well where the soil is poor.

The production process

The low-cost food processing kitchen — which was built by the village men — is a simple wooden-framed building with screened windows and concrete floor. This kitchen includes a clay/sand stove, screened cupboard, open shelves, washing basin, first-aid box and working tables. A ferro-cement water tank collects rainwater off the roof for use in processing.

Peeling is done by slitting the skins with a knife and stripping them with the fingers. The sap of the skin sticks to and stains the hand, but the villagers have found that rubbing salt on the hands reduces this problem. The peeled bananas are dropped into a bucket of salted water which helps to remove the remaining sap from the surface of the bananas. The waste skins are used for pig feed.

The peeled bananas are sliced along their length approximately 1.6mm (1/16 inch) thick. Initially, a locally made version of an imported slicer was used, consisting of a wooden board with a stainless steel blade. However, this proved to be inefficient and unhygienic. Now an imported moulded plastic unit with a stainless steel blade is used. This is quite reasonably priced and is stocked by one of the major retail stores. The banana slices are dropped straight into salted water.

Drying is recommended, as it helps to prevent the banana slices from sticking together when they are dropped into the frying oil. Undried slices take longer to fry, and cause more rapid deterioration of the oil. The banana slices are taken out of the salted water and placed on drying racks. These racks consist of plastic shade cloth, stretched over light wooden frames. Earlier, fly-wire was used but was harder to clean, broke easily and corroded. The raw banana slices do not seem to attract flies or insects, although the peel and ripe bananas do.

The drying racks are placed on shelves in the open shade. This makes it easier to control the drying process than drying in the sun, as the drying is more uniform throughout. Only a small amount of drying (an hour or so) is needed to remove the surface moisture. The women have learned to recognize when the slices are sufficently dried. Over-drying results in hard chips and poor colour.

A high oil temperature (about 230°C) is needed to get good quality crispy chips. An efficient smokeless firewood stove which is made from a clay and sand mixture has been constructed by the villagers with assistance from ATDI.

The stove contains two aluminium washing bowls used as frying

Sealing the bags using a hacksaw blade and candle flame

units. Banana slices are fried until they turn a golden brown and are then drained, cooled and dusted with salt. The salted banana chips are packed in polyethylene bags and sealed with a hacksaw blade and candle flame.

Initially, the plastic bags were sealed with only a candle flame which, although functional, did not give a neat appearance. This method was then replaced by using a commercial plastic sealer powered by a car battery. This worked well but the villagers could not maintain the sealer themselves.

When packed and sealed properly, the banana chips stay fresh and crisp for up to six weeks. Every packet is inspected to check that it is sealed properly, and then the bags are packed in second-hand cardboard boxes, sealed with tape and marked, showing the quantity and date when produced.

Marketing and management

Originally, the banana chips were sold informally through private orders and around the Situm area. At present an average of 700-1,000 bags per week are marketed under the brand name 'MR BANANA SIP' through two shops in Lae. Consumer acceptance has geen good and it seems from the report of the shop-owners that the potential demand is far higher.

The management of the enterprise follows a pattern of organization which was largely set up by the villagers themselves, based on their experience in running their own shop and piggery, and in growing cash crops. The village headman is the ultimate decision maker. His wife is the chief organizer of the production side. Their adopted son who runs the trade store looks after the bookkeeping and logistics. (It is interesting to note that none of these three receives any direct financial benefit. Profits from the enterprise go into the community account.) The Situm group has taken the first step towards formalizing the business by opening a cheque account under the name 'SIMBASI' which stands for 'Situm Banana Sip'. This is an indication of their long-term commitment to the project.

Commercial viability

When the project started the economics of production were relatively simple. Bananas were obtained from the village gardens and nearby villages. Oil, salt, plastic bags and other materials were purchased in small quantities from wholesale suppliers. Labour was more or less on a voluntary basis. As the project became more commercialized, it became clear that it was necessary to work out a buying price for bananas and to bulk purchase oil and salt to cut down the costs of materials.

Labelling became necessary to meet the Department of Labour and Industries' regulations, thus increasing the packaging costs. A scale of wages was introduced to pay the staff. Arrangements have also been made for the transport of raw materials and finished products. These steps have ensured a more regular production to meet the growing demand from urban sales outlets.

This process of development from a village pilot project to a more commercially oriented enterprise is still happening step by step. Some of the cost factors are now being assessed and calculated in a conventional businesslike manner, whereas other aspects of the costing are still affected by the village perception of customary rights and responsibilities.

At present it is difficult to say whether the enterprise is viable within the normal commercial meaning of the term. What is clear is that income is greater than expenditure, the women working in the enterprise are paid a satisfactory wage, the village economy is benefiting and the people are proud of their achievement. In the long term it seems that this enterprise could grow to become a significant local producer of snack food products. Nevertheless, if the enterprise is to retain its true village-based character, this development will be slow, as the villagers themselves gain the necessary expertise.

Food hygiene and sanitation

Both personal and food hygiene, along with sanitary working practices are vital to any food processing operation. Lack of care leads to contamination which could endanger the public. In setting up the Situm community-based food-processing enterprise, efforts have been made to ensure the hygienic quality of the products. Deep frying sterilizes the dried banana slices, and so the most vulnerable part of the process where contamination could occur is in the later steps of salting and packaging. Aprons have been supplied to all staff and are washed regularly. The women are required to wash their hands with soap before handling the chips and to wash their feet before entering the kitchen (the villagers never wear footwear). A poster is used as a reminder of the requirements of the Health Department of the Lae Interim Authority.

In general the hygiene condition is satisfactory. The people are keeping themselves and the working area clean. The sanitary education of the Situm people is no different from other aspects of the project. The approach is straightforward but gradual, to let them absorb the process of change rather than forcing them to follow a rigid set of instructions.

Conclusion

Experience with the Situm people has lead the author to realize that their business practices, which may seem unconventional, are logical in terms of their own perceptions and social structure. The group is highly motivated, socially coherent and very much committed to their own community. Community obligations are usually given priority over business activities. Nevertheless, they have been able to take a flexible approach to integrating production with their village life. Areas that could have been a problem such as non-cash incentives or payment of minimum wages, were solved step by step in an informal Melanesian way. Outside assistance has been reduced, yet the people seem to be able to handle most difficulties independently. The main need now is to increase production to meet the demand and achieve a more commercially viable scale of operations.

The Situm group has taken the initiative to teach what they have learned to interested neighbours, community groups or school children, and have participated in a number of ATDI workshops. They recently accommodated a group of people from a Sepik Women's Club and gave them on-the-job training for three weeks.

Update

Since the beginning of 1984 the author has withdrawn her direct involvement with the project. There were internal conflicts among members of the group which resulted in the voluntary departure of the manager of the project. This forced the women's leader to take on more responsibility for the business. Initially she faced many difficulties but she was determined to prove that she could handle the business, and she is now leading a production team of four to five skilled women and some boy and girl school-leavers.

The new Lorena stove is now in use and with a lot of hard work and determination the women have more than doubled their production and the chips are now on sale at one of the most well-known supermarkets in the town. The product quality is still inconsistent — this is probably the result of training new members of the production team and also the local schoolchildren who come every Friday to learn how to make chips. Customers and retailers, however, have kindly been giving feedback on the quality of the chips and the group is trying to improve it in response to this.

This, although at the time the conflict seemed unfortunate, because the author stayed out of the matter and let the villagers work out their own solution, it has actually brought some benefits, because the women have been forced to take on more responsibility for their business and production has not suffered.

The progress of the Situm project so far indicates that:
1. It is possible to carry out community-based, food processing using simple production systems and technologies.
2. It is necessary to evolve a style of production and management which will satisfy both the requirements of commercial viability and the realities of village life.

The Situm Project is being thoroughly studied and documented to be used as a possible model for other village food processing enterprises. The author's experience with the Situm people has

51

indicated certain features in project management that might be instructive to those who work in similar fields. That is, the approach must be slow but steady to allow time for the villagers to solve their own problems in their own way. Their involvement should be encouraged so that they make their own decisions and contribute their ideas, skills, time and finance towards the project. Development workers should be able to advise and take a leading role when required, but also be prepared to step back when necessary.

Further reading

Aveda, L.V., Gopez, M.D. and Payumo, E.M., 'Studies on the preparation and storage qualities of banana chips', *Philippines Journal of Science*, 97, 2735. 1968.

Bai, G.S. and Rao, M.N., 'The use of packaging and anti-oxidants in banana chipping', *Journal of Food Science Technology*, Vol.6, pp.169-172. 1969.

Bourke, R.M., 'Notes on Types of Banana', Papua New Guinea Food Crops Conference, Department of Primary Industry, Port Moresby. 1976.

Jain, N.L., Nair, K.G., Sidappa, G.S. and Lal, G., 'Studies to improve the keeping quality of fried salted banana chips', *Food Science*, Vol. 11, pp.335-38. 1962.

SMALL-SCALE FRUIT PROCESSING IN SAINT VINCENT

Barrie Axtell

In 1972, the British Government set up a series of Produce Laboratories in the Caribbean Islands of Grenada, Saint Vincent, Saint Lucia and Dominica, and at a later date, Montserrat. These units consisted of a laboratory section and a multi-purpose pilot plant, and were supplied with the books, chemicals and equipment necessary for all the analytical methods that might be needed. Each laboratory was intended to act as a technical resource for the island: carrying out the research necessary for utilization of the island's agricultural products; analysis, for example for the police and customs; and product development. The pilot plant was therefore fully equipped with a mill, drier, steam kettle, boiler and a distillation system for the extraction of essential oils from herbs and spices.

Initially, the laboratories were staffed by a British Technical Co-operation Officer, a VSO, a local counterpart and assistants,

The steam kettles in which the juice is pasteurized

53

but they are now totally run and funded by the governments of the individual island states.

The basic economy of the eastern Caribbean islands is agricultural, and in many cases it was found that they were exporting their raw materials and then importing similar processed products from outside at considerable expense. Aiming to prevent this, the laboratories concentrated their research on food-processing techniques that would lead to import substitution. In Saint Vincent, for example, some twenty-five products were developed and marketed, including fruit drinks, jams, chutneys and sauces. Despite the fact that the processing systems were made freely available to any local entrepreneur who expressed interest, few took advantage of the advice and techniques offered to them. The two main problems were marketing and capital investment. It was generally felt that the locally made goods could not compete with the prestigious, sophisticatedly packaged, imported items. To try and overcome this, some of the pilot plants were turned into regular production units which sold their produce to local supermarkets and, in the case of Saint Vincent, exported a small amount to Barbados and even to Canada. At the same time, research into packaging, new products and marketing was continued.

The Orange Hill Plant

In 1983, a local entrepreneur, the owner of the Orange Hill Estates in Saint Vincent, became interested in the laboratory's work and decided to set up a production unit with the help of its expertise. Initially, the investment was very low, about 150 to 200, and lime juice cordial was produced in an ordinary kitchen at a production rate of only twenty-four bottles a day. This limited production, however, allowed test marketing and costings to be carried out. On the strength of these results, the investment was increased to around 500 and a small room was converted to a production centre which was able to produce some 100 packs a day and within two years the results were sufficiently encouraging to lay down a proper production unit. Output now runs up to 2,000 packs per day, depending on the product, and a canning line for grapefruit juice has been added. The products of the Orange Hill Estates are well known in local hotels and supermarkets, and have virtually replaced equivalent imported items. There is also a regular export trade to Barbados.

Today, ten year later, the plant employs about fifteen people and is mainly supplied with produce from the owner's estate. The

Glueing on the labels by hand

processes are comparatively simple — the manufacture of grapefruit juice is an example.

After washing, the fruit is cut in half by hand and the two halves are held against a machine-driven rose to extract the juice. A known quantity of this juice is then put into a steam kettle (the steam being provided by a diesel-fired boiler which is probably the greatest cost in the plant) together with sugar syrup, and it is heated to pasteurize it. The grapefruit is then pumped to a header tank from which hot juice may be dispensed into the tin cans below. Empty cans, after washing, are put on to the circular filling table and the operator spins the table-top around, filling each can in turn and then presenting it to the hand can-seaming machine where the lid is fitted. The hot sealed cans are then rolled down a wooden conveyor into a bath of chlorinated cold water to cool them. They are removed by hand and allowed to roll by gravity along another conveyor, through which warm air is blown, provided by hair driers and an electric fan. Labels are attached to the dry cans using a small hand-glueing machine. Much of the equipment was made in the Orange Hill Estates workshops.

The production levels of the Orange Hill Estates in Saint Vincent remain virtually the same as in 1976, possibly because the home market has been more or less saturated, and although there is interest in Canada and the United States, the orders from these markets are far too large for their small company to fill. In order to break into the larger export markets, the laboratories in the different islands would have to co-operate, thus reducing costs by bulk-buying imported material such as pectin and packaging, and producing a limited number of lines to a standard recipe so that they could jointly fulfill large orders. This approach might allow increased production without having to intensify traditional agricultural methods or having to resort to highly capital-intensive automatic equipment, and would provide a considerable number of jobs. The plant employs mostly women, and working there is considered far preferable to digging arrowroot or splitting coconuts — the other job alternatives. Such a step would also bring in foreign exchange to the islands, but at the same time would place them in the position of becoming involved in the uncertainty of international markets.

There is little doubt that the Orange Hill Estates in Saint Vincent owe their success partly to a government ban which was placed on imported products. This gave them access to a market, with shopkeepers eager to take locally produced goods in order to maintain stocks.

A technical resource centre

At the local level, the Orange Hill project is a notable success in the transfer of technology, and some useful lessons can be learned from it. First, there is no doubt that the laboratory-cum-pilot plant complex was an essential catalyst. Previous attempts to establish small food industries had tended to be unsuccessful, as there was little technical resource back-up or expertise on production techniques, formulations, the use of preservatives, costings and market research. The laboratory was able to assist small producers in overcoming comparatively simple problems that required some basic technical work.

The Saint Vincent laboratory, now renamed the Agrolab, served the community in other ways, too. Home economics courses were run in the villages in the evenings, offering benefits to the village women, and advice was given to the few existing small-scale food processing industries. An attempt was made to set up a system of producing orange juice, which at that time was being imported in cans from Trinidad.

In Saint Vincent there is little, or no, orchard production of oranges; farmers tend to have a few trees in their backyard. It is generally not really worthwhile for these small producers to bring a few oranges into the town to sell, so the Agrolab set up a system of going around the villages on a well-publicized schedule to buy the fruit. A folding table, on which were mounted several orange juice squeezing machines, was taken out in their van and several village ladies employed as workers. The fruit was purchased on site, washed and then squeezed with hand presses, the juice being collected in large plastic barrels. After adding a preservative, this raw juice could be taken back to the plant for processing. This system provided an on-site market for farmers for small quantities of fruit, saving the time and expense of a trip to the city market, provided a day's work for a few villagers in weighing and squeezing the fruit, and to the advantage of the Agrolab, left the fruit waste in the village where it could perhaps be better disposed of.

Unfortunately, the laboratories on their own were not sufficient to promote development. The investment required to begin even minimal production, and the risk of competing with imported goods, meant that most small entrepreneurs could not take advantage of the resources and the support the laboratories had to offer. To expand production to the next stage, a resident entrepreneur with capital and suitable facilities was necessary. It so happened that the owner of the Orange Hill Estates had the necessary buildings and a steam boiler available, and, having his own raw materials, wished to diversify. Obviously, as the Orange Hill plant was a private company, the owner's commitment to it was strong and a lot of his energy and inventiveness is evident in his plant.

Finally, as mentioned before, government support is crucial to the success of small-scale local industries. Had there not been a ban on imported goods at the time that the Orange Hill plant started production, its products might not have been able to establish themselves in the local market. Here, at least, small island states, such as Saint Vincent, have the advantage. Import control is easier and bureaucracy is less of an obstacle to legislation. On one occasion when the supply of old beer bottles for the laboratory was threatened by the establishment of a brewery on a nearby island which started to buy back the bottles at a higher price, a crisis was averted by immediate legislation banning the export of old beer bottles! This kind of prompt and supportive government action is absolutely critical if small island communities are to take advantage of their natural isolation and small scale to increase their self-sufficiency through the development of local small-scale industries.

RECIPES FOR INDEPENDENCE

Jessica Barry

Since the British withdrew from Belize in 1981, small income-generating projects have been springing up at a local level all over the country. Most of them are being run by women, and they indicate how self-motivated and determined the women are to use the familiar things which are part of their daily lives, in new and profitable ways.

Banana flour

Plantains are one of the two main cash crops being grown in the area (the other is cassava), and they can be made into banana flour. Some time ago, a group of women from the village of Independence set up a project to do this on a small commercial scale. They got help from the Women's Bureau in Belize City to start the project and began selling the flour in one pound (450g) bags.

To make banana flour, green plantains are first peeled and sliced, and are then spread out on sheets of galvanized zinc to dry in the sun. When they have become crisp they are gathered up and ground into a fine flour. In its processed state it is called *concante*, and can be used in place of ordinary flour to make cakes and puddings.

Dried fruits

A number of other women living in Independence came together last year and formed a Women and Development Group to set up a business using solar heat to dry local fruit, such as mangoes, pineapples and papayas. They were prompted to do this by the fact that a lot of the produce grown by local farmers was being wasted, since the dirt road leading from the village to Dangriga, the nearest town, was often impassable after heavy rain.

There is not a great demand for dried fruit in Belize so, with a keen business sense, the group decided to aim for the expanding health food industry in the United States. A Peace Corps volunteer, Juliet Mason, who was working locally on the

Strategies

1. Undertake a thorough market survey with a wide range of potential customers.

2. Utilize the services of technicians and scientists who will advise on quality control and product development.

3. Pinpoint the advantages you can offer the consumer over other companies.

Idea Bank

DOING A SIMPLE MARKET SURVEY:

1. DETERMINE YOUR MARKET...Do you plan to reach the local population, the whole country, specific sectors (i.e., the tourist industry, women, teenagers, etc.)?

2. SURVEY THE COMPETITION...How do their prices compare with yours? How does their quality control compare with yours? Why would people buy your product instead of theirs?

3. DO A MARKET TEST...Ask people to test and offer feedback on your product; produce a small quantity to offer in local markets; record how they were received.

4. EVALUATE THE RESULTS OF STEPS #1 - 3...Modify your production process, pricing, quality control, advertising and distribution plans accordingly.

Some suggestions from the International Women's Tribune Centre on setting up a small business and identifying the market

development of appropriate technologies, helped them to get the project under way.

First of all they built a demonstration solar dryer using local wood and a simple design taken from an appropriate technology manual. They adapted it slightly to suit their own particular needs; for example, making it tall enough to be used at waist height, for that was how most of the women prepared and cooked their food at home. They also made provision for a wood fire underneath the dryer to supplement the heat from the solar panel. The hottest season in Belize is also the wettest, which makes the drying of uncovered food a lengthy process. Because the solar dryer is enclosed, however, food can be left in it even when it is raining, and the heat can be maintained if there is not much sun, by lighting the back-up fire.

The next step was to find out how to tell when the fruit was dry enough. This was done either by weighing it (it was dry enough once it had lost a third of its original weight), or by leaving it in the heat until it reached a predetermined density of colour, at which point it was ready for the final process, which was to preserve it using either honey or sugar.

Until now, the women have financed the project themselves by making handicrafts, giving barbecues and putting on entertainments in the village. The success of the business depends, however, on finding a stable market, and until this is done it will not be possible to judge how profitable the scheme might become in the long term. The eventual aim is to set up a revolving fund financed from the profit on sales, and to be totally independent.

LEAF PROTEIN — A SIMPLE TECHNOLOGY TO IMPROVE NUTRITION

Ann Maddison and Glyn Davys

Lunawa is a coastal village in the southern area of Sri Lanka where the children can be seen to eat fortified *kola kenda* regularly. This local porridge traditionally made from coconut, rice and the juice from fresh green leaves, began to be repopularized by the rural development group Sarvodaya in its nursery schools during the spread of malnutrition after the 1973 cyclone. The traditional pestle and mortar was a tedious tool for the pulping of green leaves from which the juice was squeezed out by hand before including in the *kola kenda*. On hearing of Find Your Feet's work on leaf protein, Sarvodaya enquired about a more efficient juice extraction method. As many villages have no electricity, Find Your Feet had a prototyle pedal-powered juice extractor made in India and commissioned it in 1982, at Lunawa, where it is still in regular daily use.

To make the leaf protein, fresh green leaves are placed into the machine through a feed hopper, and are gradually moved along by a helical screw whilst at the same time being pulped and then pressed to separate out the inedible fibre from the juice. The lower part of the cylindrical outer casing is perforated to allow the juice to be squeezed out into a container in which it is placed on a fire and heated until a coagulum forms. At this stage the pot is taken off the fire and the contents poured through a muslin bag to filter out the curd. This is washed clean with water and the resulting green product is leaf protein.

Adding leaf protein to the cooked rice and coconut makes fortified *kola kenda* which is nutritionally superior to the traditional dish, particularly in protein, vitamin A and iron. The fortified porridge still keeps the same taste and appearance. Dr Beatric de Mel of the Medical Research Institute, Colombo, reported from analysis that *kola kenda* contained normally 1-2g protein in a 200ml portion. Of this the leaf juice would contribute about 0.1g protein plus about 0.25mg of beta-carotene (a precursor of vitamin A), whereas the leaf protein concentrate

Find Your Feet's original prototype pedal-powered juice extractor, in use since 1982

provided the children with 4-5g of protein and 12mg of beta-carotene.

The mothers were so pleased with the improvement in their children's health and growth that it was decided to make the preparation of fortified *kola kenda* standard practice. In January 1987 a team under Professor Priyani Soysa (Head of the Department of Paediatrics, University of Colombo, and a member of the WHO Committee on Nutrition) surveyed the Lunawa children in comparison with a similar group in another Sarvodaya pre-school about a mile away; the latter group's treatment had been the same in all respects except that they had had the

Producing the helical screw which will move the green leaves along while they are being pulped

traditional as opposed to the fortified *kola kenda*. The conclusion was that the Lunawa children's health was dramatically better.

Spread of the technology among villages

Since the introduction of the first leaf extraction machine which was pedal powered, a hand-operated machine has been developed, and is being produced locally for distribution throughout the Sarvodaya system. To date the use of leaf-protein extraction technology and its incorporation into the local diets has spread to about 30 villages in Sri Lanka. This is just the beginning, for the Prime Minister has said that it should be available for mass distribution at every child health centre on the island.

The hand-powered leaf protein extractor partly assembled

Although there is no commercial element at the Sarvodaya nursery schools, Find Your Feet views the introduction of leaf-protein technology as having a potential for an income-generating activity because the two by-products involved — fibre to process into animal feed and a sugary liquor to use as a substitute for fermentation (for example, for alcohol) or as a fertilizer — can be manufactured to provide a cash income.

The proliferation of leaf-protein production in Sri Lanka for use as a food for people has come about both due to a change in women's processing techniques, and the gradual realization that the improved levels of nutrition effectively combats many long-term and painful symptoms of protein malnutrition (kwashiorkor), vitamin A deficiency (xeropthalmia) and iron deficiency (anaemia). Such success may be attributed in part to the fact that ways have been found to introduce a food and a technology in a manner that local communities have adopted and decided to spread.

IMPROVING THE TRADITIONAL GHANAIAN BAKING OVEN

G. Campbell Platt

In Ghana, the baking of bread is mostly a small-scale industry, with over 19,000 women bakers recorded in the most recent population census.[1] Imported wheat is milled into white flour at the country's ports in large, modern, capital-intensive mills, and this is distributed in sacks throughout the country to the women bakers. The traditional oven is dome-shaped, built from sun-dried or fired clay bricks and covered with a clay coating on the outside. Firewood is introduced through the opening of the oven and is burnt to heat the oven to about 300°C, estimated by feeling the heat on the outside surface of the oven. Any remaining unburnt wood or ash is drawn out, and the oven is allowed to cool for about ten minutes after which the temperature drops to about 240°C. The trays or tins of proved dough are then inserted into the base of the oven, the opening is closed with a wooden or corrugated iron door and the bread is baked in the residual heat of the oven. Baking takes 20 to 25 minutes, and the oven can usually be reloaded and a second batch of bread baked without further heating.

Why build an improved traditional oven?

At the Nutrition and Food Science Department of the University of Ghana, students are trained in nutrition and in food science, which has generally been oriented towards medium- and large-scale food processing. However, Ghana's main food processors operate low-capital, small-scale processing plant, such as the traditional baking oven. One of the steps taken to ensure that the University's food science students make a contribution to small-scale food processing has been the establishment of a Nutrition and Food Science Society. This aims to involve the lecturers and students in a wider education beyond the campus. The Society's first project was to build an improved traditional oven in the grounds of the University department, and to use it to bake wholemeal bread for sale. By baking wholemeal bread, not only is there nutritional advantage over white bread, but Ghana's scarce but Ghana's scarce foreign exchange is conserved as all the imported wheat is milled into flour rather than the usual extraction rate of 75 per cent for white flour.

Design of the oven

To improve heat retention, fired bricks were used in the construction of the oven walls and base. The bricks were held together with clay containing salt, and the base of the oven was filled with broken glass. These features allow more baking to be carried out for the same initial quantity of firewood. The major design feature of this improved oven, which allows a doubling of the capacity of the traditional one, is the inclusion of a shelf in the oven. The oven was built on campus by a mason who regularly builds traditional ovens.

Extension of the improved oven

The idea of doubling the capacity of the oven by incorporating a shelf can only be regarded as a success when other bakers take up the idea. The plan is for the all-important extension to work in three ways.[2]

Through the mason

By employing a mason who regularly builds ovens, the idea can be passed on by him to other bakers. This aim is already being attained. When constructing the oven, the mason had to stand on the base and build it around himself. He was not happy about having to stand astride the iron rods to continue the building and after much heated discussion (and some tense moments) he agreed to the incorporation of the shelf. Later, at the commissioning ceremony watched by enthusiastic students and staff, the mason poured libation to the ancestors and said that he realized what an advantage the shelf was, and that he was going to build his next oven the same way!

Through the women

The second approach has been to involve the women bakers through the close involvement of the National Council on Women and Development in the project. The participants at a NCWD foreign exchange is conserved as all the imported wheat is milled into flour rather than the usual extraction rate of 75 per cent for white flour.

Woman baker in Ghana

Wholemeal bread

Thirdly, the oven is being used to bake and sell wholemeal bread,
which is now very much in demand. Some of the customers, or
their wives, are the small-scale bakers to whom this project is
directed and it hoped that they will take up the idea in their own
baking activities.

Appropriateness

The improved oven can be built anywhere, even in rural areas
where electricity is not available. The oven is similar in external
appearance to the traditional oven which is well known in Ghana;
this familiarity should make it readily acceptable. The improved

oven will take one hundred 500 gram loaves, 50 on the base and 50 on the shelf, as against only 50 which could be accommodated on the floor of the normal oven of the same size.

The oven conserves fuel wood, giving twice the quantity of bread for the same initial quantity of wood. In Ghana, as in many developing countries, firewood is scarce and costly. The attraction of being able to obtain twice as much bread for the same amount of fuel is immediate and obvious to the woman baker, and is a saving to the country's stocks of energy. In the long term, perhaps the most important aspect of the improved traditional oven is the involvement of the food science and nutrition degree students. After graduating, students will now feel able to play an important role both in the larger-scale food industries and small-scale food processing. With so many people, both producers and consumers, dependent on traditional small-scale food processing in Ghana, the country needs the involvement of food science graduates in developing appropriate food technologies for everyone's benefit.

References

1. Youngs, A.J. (1972) 'Wheat flour and bread consumption in West Africa: A review with special reference to Ghana', *Tropical Science 14*, pp.235-44.
2. Youngs, A.J. (1984) 'Developing countries need food technology extension'. *Food Technology 27*, pp.97-104.

CASSAVA CRISPBREAD

Jessica Barry

The women of Hopkins, Belize, have turned to their cultural roots to find a means of financial support. Theirs is a Garifuna community, an ethnic group of mixed African and Amerindian descent, whose forebears came to Belize from the West Indies at the beginning of the nineteenth century. They maintain their unique language and distinctive customs even today. An integral part of their life-style is the making of cassava bread, and in the same way that the women in Independence (also a Garifuna community) are using plantains, the women in Hopkins are using the other traditional staple of their diet, cassava, and are processing it to bring themselves an income.

A group of thirteen women and two men have been making cassava bread on a small commercial scale in the village for the past three years. Bitter cassava (manioc) is used, and must be picked only a day in advance or else it will spoil. The root is peeled using a paring knife (Figure 1), then washed and grated on a mahogany board studded with quartz stones (Figure 2). The grated cassava is placed in a *wahla* (named after a snake) — a

Peeling the cassava

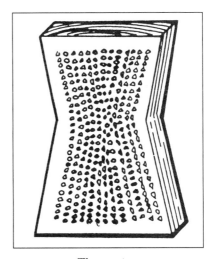

The grater

69

long basket-weave tube with a hoop at each end. The *wahla* is hung up on a branch of a stout tree and a pole or wooden board is inserted through the bottom hoop. Two people sit on it (Figure 3), thus stretching the tube and extracting the excess juices and starch. These are collected in a bowl and can be used to make pressing starch, or a gruel. The cassava is sifted through a large sieve made from coconut palm leaves. This separates the fine cassava powder which will be used for bread, from the shredded remains which are fed to animals. A wood fire is lit under a two-foot diameter *camal* (iron baking tray) which is raised on blocks six inches off the ground. When the *camal* is hot, damp cassava powder is sprinkled over its surface, patted down with a flat board, and brushed with a whisk-type broom made from salt water pimento leaves (Figure 4). The bread is turned over after five minutes and more cassava powder is brushed on to it to smooth the surface. The bread is then scored with a machete into a grid pattern, and turned around several times. When it begins to brown, it is taken off the *camal* and placed on sheets of galvanized zinc to dry out in the sun. Last of all it is packed up into plastic bags and taken to Belize City where it is sold from door to door for B$2 (US$1) per pound. The finished product resembles a thin crispbread and keeps indefinitely.

This tiny local enterprise is a good example of the way in which many Belizean women are becoming self reliant, and are using tasks which form part of their daily lives for a new purpose. By creating successful schemes with the simple materials that are readily available to them, they are able to expand their horizons and enjoy the prospect of gaining an income — however small.

Squeezing the grated cassava in the wahla

Cooking the crispbread on the camal *over a woodfire*

WOMEN AND FISH-SMOKING
Ruby Sandhu

A technology can never be looked at in isolation from the community it is designed to serve. The introduction of any new or improved technology should be in answer to demands expressed by the users. However, while the user's needs are taken into consideration during the initial design and development stage, or at the pilot stage, the diffusion of the technology to a larger audience faces many obstacles. This chapter will look specifically at the introduction of an improved fish-smoking technology, the chorkor, and its spread among the coastal communities of West Africa. The social, economic, technical and political aspects of the chorkor's introduction which have either helped or hindered its diffusion on a wider scale will be discussed.

Fish processing and the community

Before considering the chorkor smoker and its technical merits, it is necessary to look at where fish processing falls within the structure of a community to understand its importance to that community. In most places, fish processing (whether it is smoking, salting or drying) is a social system as well as a livelihood. The social organization or the division of labour is already fixed.

By and large, fishing is the domain of men, while processing belongs to women; although in some fishing villages men also do the processing, usually by smoking. The relationships between the suppliers (the fishermen) and the processors, have long been established. There are two most common types of relationships; in the first, the husband fishes exclusively for his wife, who processes the catch. The fisherman then sells it. In the other case, there may be no family link between the fisherman and the processor, and he sells his fish to anyone who can pay his price. These links also define whether the fisherman is the sole owner of the boat or owns it collectively, in which case either the fish catch is divided, or the proceeds from its sale. Moreover, in countries where there has never been a strong fishing tradition, in Togo, for example, the women are forced to rely on foreign fishermen (usually Ghanaian), who come to fish seasonally. These men supply almost exclusively those women who 'hire' them, and often provide them with room and board.

Women filling top tray of the stack. The fuel hole is stoked with wood and coconut husks

In terms of purchasing the fish, sometimes women buy the fish (from their husbands or the fishermen), process the fish and then sell it. Alternatively, the women pay the fishermen only after they have sold the processed fish, in this way the fishermen profit from the higher price that processed fish fetches. Another arrangement is that a woman will sometimes pay for a fisherman's trip, by paying for the outboard fuel, and in return, the catch from that particular trip belongs to that woman. These are only a few of the relationships that exist between the fishermen and the processor. Clearly, any change, be it an improvement or not, may alter these relationships and make it more difficult for the people concerned to accept a new technology.

Women and technology

Changes in fishing technology will affect women in processing because the activities are interdependent. Any changes in fishing will directly affect women's workload, and the delicate balance of the production cycle. For example, in a project in Sierra Leone, where improvements were introduced both to fishing and to processing, the women were very concerned that increased

72

The cleaned fish are spread out on the tray, and ready for smoking to begin

productivity would lead to the fishing grounds becoming overfished. The women preferred a well-regulated operation which ensured a regular income.[1]

The major problems raised in the small-scale or artisanal fishing industry concern not only the processing methods, such as a need for an improved smoker which uses less fuel, but also the fishing methods. Many small-scale fishermen cannot compete against other fishermen who own engine-powered boats which enable them to fish farther out, increase their catch and dominate the fish-processing market.

Thus, the introduction of an improved oven which allowed women to smoke more fish, would be pointless without a corresponding rise in the fish supply. Such situations dampen the spirits of the women and can result in the rejection of a technology which appears to be useful. The implication is that a new technology, such as a smoking oven, cannot be introduced without considering all the other inter-related activities. The user must be concerned not only with how a new technology will affect her relationship with the fisherman. These links in the community, whether they are between fishermen and fishwives or supplier and processor need to be examined in order to see where — in terms of the entire picture — an improvement will fit.

A woman filleting and cleaning her fish before smoking

The chorkor in Ghana

Physically, the chorkor is a rectangular oven with two stoke holes in the front. Ideally, a foundation is sunk into the ground and a dividing wall creates two smaller cooking spaces (both are recent improvements on earlier models). The chorkor is designed so that the wooden frames of the trays will rest along the mud ridges of the oven walls. The smoker has a large capacity: up to 18 kilos of fish per tray, and as many as 15 trays can be used per oven.

In Ghana, the chorkor has had a very high acceptance rate because its design corresponds very closely to the traditional smoker, differing only in that trays can be stacked allowing a greater number of fish to be smoked at one time. Because the chorkor is virtually a completely closed system with the trays acting as a type of chimney, it uses less fuel and the heat is more evenly distributed. Charring occurs less often because the fire can be controlled better. Although the introduction of the chorkor in Ghana allowed the women to increase the amount of fish smoked, significantly, its acceptance was due also to its similarity to traditional methods. Indeed, some women in Ghana found that fish smoked using the chorkor commanded a higher price in the market. They also noticed that many women would buy fish smoked by the chorkor in preference to the traditionally smoked fish.

It is a general rule that there is greater motivation for people to accept an improved income-generating technology than one used only for domestic purposes. The reasoning behind this is that as women often use firewood for their commercial activities (e.g. brewing and baking) and as this firewood must be bought, a significant reduction in consumption would lower production costs. And, a woman who already has a source of income is more likely to be able to buy new equipment or get a loan independently of her husband.

If improved technologies are available, and if the motivation to use them also exists, why then is their use limited? One of the reasons already mentioned is that of a lack of raw materials. For example, as a result of the success of the chorkor, the Ghanaian National Council on Women and Development granted women loans in order to purchase the chorkors. These loans were repaid rapidly because of the profitability of the chorkor. Unfortunately, fishermen could not meet the processors' increased demand for fish as their methods were still traditional.[2]

A second reason why the technology may not be adapted is because women may not have physical access to the technology. The women or the local artisans may not be able to replicate the chorkor to its exact dimensions in which case the technology loses its effectiveness. Artisans from neighbouring villages may be interested in learning how to build the oven, and facilities for training them are needed. In Ghana, carpenters from other villages copied the chorkor fish smoker from the original factory model, but sometimes they got the dimensions and clay mixture wrong. The ovens cracked and the trays caught fire. This happened not only in Ghana, but also in other neighbouring countries where access to the original factory is even more difficult.

Obviously, this type of publicity or dissemination only hinders the acceptance of a technology and greatly reduces its credibility.

One of the main advantages of the chorkor is that the trays can be stacked to allow women to smoke up to 15 trays of fish. Although up to 15 trays can be used, one rarely sees more than six or seven in use. Why are the women not fully exploiting the capacity of the chorkor? The first reason has already been mentioned: they do not have enough fish. Secondly, when the trays are full, they are heavy and difficult to manage, so the women must organize work teams. Consequently, tests are needed to ensure that when only six or seven trays are used the

A woman who has adapted her traditional oven by covering the sides to save fuel — the technique used by the chorkor

oven does not lose its chimney effect and stop being fuel-efficient.

A further reason why usually only six or seven trays are used at a time relates to the way the fish are placed on the tray. For example, in business it was discovered that the fish is smoked by placing it on its side or head, in this way large quantities of fish can be smoked at one time. While with the new chorkor, fish is placed flat on the trays, which greatly reduced the amount that could be smoked. The women tried smoking the fish by placing it on its side in the trays, but the trays were not deep enough and the fish got crushed. Moreover, when this type of fish was being smoked flat, it would break apart. Even so, the Guinean women were quick to see the advantage of the chorkor in that it was a closed fire whereas their traditional ovens were completely open. (The traditional oven is like a long table with wooden legs and a metal or wire-mesh grill.) Consequently, the women have returned to their traditional ovens, but they have covered the sides with sheet-metal in order to increase the fuel-efficiency of the oven. At the same time, they are also trying to increase the depth of the chorkor trays so that they can use it.

In this case, although the chorkor was not completely

The traditional chorkor is a long table, open underneath where the fire is built. The fish are stacked tightly together on their sides

satisfactory, the women did get certain advantages from the chorkor and modified their traditional techniques to get better fuel-efficiency. More importantly, others in the villages and outside have made similar changes to their traditional ovens. In one Guinean village where both men and women smoke fish, a chorkor was given to some women, who then adapted their traditional ovens. The men followed suit immediately in order to be more fuel-efficient as well.

Designs must build on the familiar

One of the major considerations when designing a new technology is the traditional method. Ideally, the improved technology should build on the traditional method. Often, if a new technology is significantly different from a traditional one it can be rejected because the users may not understand the advantages. Fuel-efficiency alone will not necessarily motivate people; the user has to see an economic advantage.

The chorkor has many advantages which make it an improvement. Similarly, there are also problems. For example, while the chorkor has an increased capacity of about 250kg, it is

77

rarely used to this capacity, but smokes roughly the same amount of fish as the traditional oven. On the other hand, users do get fuel savings and people prefer the taste of the fish smoked this way.

This article has attempted to point out that many factors — social, economic and political — play a part in the acceptance and dissemination of a technology. A technology must never be looked at in isolation, for it will be introduced into a community whose work patterns, social arrangements and traditional beliefs have evolved over a long period. Any effective introduction of an improved technology must begin with an understanding of the various activities and organization. Efficiency and economic profitability are not the only factors influencing the acceptance of a new method, but also compatibility to peoples' habitual patterns of doing their work.

References

1. Filonania Chioma Stead, 'Women's Work in Rural Cash Food Systems: The Tombo and Gloucester Development Projects, Sierra Leone', in *Rural Development and Women: lessons from the field*, Shimwaayi Muntemba, ed., ILO, 1985.
2. Eugenia Date-Bah, 'Constraints to technological improvements in rural women's activities', *Vrouwen in de derde werdd energie en clange paste technologie, Brouwenstudies teksten III.*

WOMEN AND BEEKEEPING

Margaret Nixon

Beekeeping is an excellent self-help activity world-wide; it is particularly important in tropical and sub-tropical areas where it can help to meet the urgent needs of the rural populations by providing nutrition, more income, and good opportunities for gainful employment. Although beekeeping has traditionally been men's work in many societies, more women are now keeping bees in Africa, Asia and Latin America. Women already carry out a large proportion of the agricultural work in many countries, including the preparation and sale of food for market. Many aspects of bee management and the marketing of bee products make beekeeping especially attractive for women: commitment can be variable, from a few hives close to home, to full-time work; it does not compete with resources from other agricultural activities; it can be done with little financial input, and the income can be used directly to help the family.

Beekeeping need not be heavy work; the top-bar hives now used in Kenya, and the *Apis cerana* colonies in Asia are small and

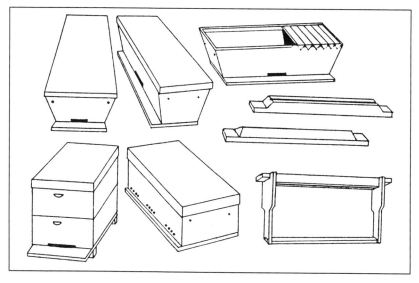

Beehives, top bars and frames

79

easy to handle. Work can also be shared by forming beekeeping co-operatives. The following is an example of a women's co-operative in Honduras, where beekeeping is one of many activities being undertaken by village women.

The co-operative was established with advice from the Honduras Ministry of Natural Resources in 1981, and with a bank loan which had to be repaid within 4 to 5 years.

The co-operative of 18 women and 2 boys receive regular advice from a Ministry project co-ordinator. They were initially given a training course in beekeeping at their village by the government education authority. With the money from the bank loan, a honey-extracting house (including water on tap), and 34 colonies in Langstroth hives, were established. The members divided into three groups which carry out in turn the necessary management for a ten-day period, paying themselves the equivalent of the average (male) daily wage for their labour. The Ministry project co-ordinator gives assistance to each group, especially advice on finances. The only written records kept at the moment, by the elected Secretary, are the financial accounts. The extracted honey is sold locally, and the remaining comb honey is used by the women themselves. The beeswax is recycled by making it into a foundation which is given to the bees to draw out into comb for honey storage. The first year's honey harvest was very promising, well above the national average, and allowed the women to pay back a large proportion of the bank loan.

Encouragement and the education of women to become beekeepers should be given special attention in development programmes, because of the many advantages. Information on women's involvement in beekeeping is being co-ordinated by the advisory officer for tropical apiculture at the International Bee Research Association, who is also interested to receive details about beekeeping projects for women, whether co-operative or independent; adaptation of beekeeping equipment and how beekeeping fits into daily life.

Note

The address of IBRA is: 18, North Road, Cardiff, CF1 3DY, UK.

THE SMALL-SCALE EXPELLING OF SUNFLOWER SEED OIL

T.W. Hammonds, R.V. Harris and N. MacFarlane

The need

The Oilseeds Section of the British Tropical Development and Research Institute (TDRI) receives frequent enquiries from individuals, aid agencies and governments in developing countries on the local need for small-scale edible oil production. Correspondence and visits to developing countries make it clear that although there is a trend for developing countries to establish large modern edible-oil production factories, the case for complementary small-scale equipment is often strong. The reasons for this are complex and differ in detail from case to case. Basically, however, the further away one is from the centralized factory, the harder it is to buy vegetable oil and when, or if, it is available, it is very expensive. It seems that the costs and logistics of seed collection and the distribution of oil from a centralized plant can often outweigh the advantages of the economies of scale to the point that small-scale oil production becomes an attractive possibility.

Recognizing the potential value of small-scale oil extraction equipment to developing countries, the TDRI discussed specifications for a small expeller with Simon-Rosedowns, a UK engineering company with a long tradition in the manufacture of large oil extraction machinery, and subsequently took charge of a prototype expeller for evaluation.

Trials in Zambia

On completion of this work the TDRI was asked to try out the expeller in Zambia using sunflower seed as the oilseed. The site selected for the trials in Zambia was a Tobacco Board outstation at Mulilima, a village about twenty miles south of Serenje in Central Province. Sunflower cultivation was being encouraged as a cash crop in the area, and the trials were to be part of the Integrated Rural Development Programme financed by British Aid. The expeller was to be powered by a diesel engine rather than three-phase, 440-volt electricity because the latter was not available at the site. The high hull content of the Zambian sunflower seed (forty-four per cent) led to the decision to use a seven horsepower (hp) engine diesel engine to make sure there was enough power available to cope with this high-fibre oilseed. The prototype expeller in the pilot plant in the UK had been powered by a three horsepower, three-phase electric motor.

During October to December 1982 the expeller package was shipped to Zambia and installed and commissioned at the Mulilima Tobacco Board outstation by a TDRI oilseed technologist. At the site, the expeller was housed in a purpose-built lean-to building, which included ventilation for the diesel exhaust fumes, a store for spares and sunflower seed oil, and another store for sunflower seed and oilcake. The seed used in the trials came from the local Agricultural Marketing Board depot. The local staff consisted of an expeller operator and two labourers, each of whom was given on-the-job training.

After a number of experiments, conditions were established for flood-feeding the expeller with sunflower-seed, and opening the choke fairly wide to give an oilcake of about 3 to 4mm thickness. Before expelling, the seed was sieved to remove trash, including small stones and sand.

The oil obtained immediately after expelling was black in colour because it contained a fine suspension of seed particles. Experiments showed that leaving this oil in a forty-five gallon drum for several days allowed these fine seed particles to settle, and a clear yellow oil was produced.

Local demand

By now the crucial stage of the project had been reached: finding out the local reaction to the edible oil produced. Workers at the Tobacco Board outstation tasted the oil and all agreed it had an acceptable taste. The swiftness of what followed surprised us. By word of mouth, news spread quickly around the local villages that a good edible sunflower oil was being produced locally and within a few days there were eager queues of villagers wanting to buy it. The distribution and, importantly, packing of the oil thus produced no problems; the villagers brought their own cups, plastic bottles and even plastic bags in which to put their purchase.

The oilcake found a ready market with local commercial farmers as a component of livestock feed during the dry season when grass is in short supply.

The Mini 40 expeller in action in Zambia

The expeller has now been operated by local counterparts for twelve months since our return to TDRI and the following performance data was recorded:

Average amount of seed processed per operating day   277kg
Average oil output per operating day   50 litres
Average cake output per operating day   214kg
Average fuel consumption per operating day   3.7 litres

In general one can produce about nine litres of clarified oil from each fifty-kilogram bag of seed.

The local sunflower seed has a low oil content of only twenty-four to twenty-eight per cent. Thus 277kg of seed contains between seventy-two and eighty-four litres of oil of which fifty are recovered for sale. Further experiments on heating the seed before expelling, and on recycling the residual sediment left after oil clarification, might evolve techniques for increasing the yield of saleable oil.

Future development

A TDRI oilseed technologist has now been posted to Zambia and several additional expellers have been supplied to other farmers' co-operatives in the area as part of the British Government Aid Programme. Research and development work will be done to try to enhance the yield of oil from sunflower seed and to examine the potential of the expeller for processing other locally available oilseeds such as soya-beans and groundnuts.

One important aspect that remains to be decided is the administrative system under which the edible oil extraction facility can best be operated. Since the farmers at present regard sunflower as a cash crop they are generally anxious to sell it all at the time of harvest. The owners of the expeller would therefore, as things stand at present, have to purchase a whole year's supply of seed at harvest time and this would require a great deal of money. Possibly the Marketing Board, which currently buys the whole crop, can be persuaded to retain some at the local depots instead of selling it immediately to the central factory. Smaller quantities could then be sold throughout the year to a small expeller operator.

Another approach being examined is to persuade the farmers to keep back some seed themselves to sell to the small expeller operator to provide cash at other times of the year. A variation on this would be the so-called 'custom milling' concept whereby the farmer brings small quantities of seed to the expeller facility for extraction when he requires edible oil either for his own use or to sell to other villagers. No cash fee would be charged for the extraction, the farmer would be given the oil, but the oilcake would be kept by the mill operator as his payment, for subsequent sale to livestock owners. In this way the mill operator would at no stage need to buy the seed, nor would he own the oil. Such a procedure is widely used in the small-scale rice-milling industry with the milled grain being returned to the farmer, and the miller retaining the bran as his payment.

Note

Since this case study was written, TDRI has become the Overseas Development Natural Resources Institute (ODNRI).

SOURCES

The case studies in this collection first appeared as journal articles as follows:

Traditional paddy husking — an appropriate technology under pressure
Appropriate Technology vol. 7 no. 2 1980

A huller for producing unpolished rice
Appropriate Technology vol. 6 no. 3 1979

Successfully producing sorghum
Appropriate Technology vol. 12 no. 1 1985

Storing grain on the farm
Appropriate Technology vol. 14 no. 2 1987

Cottage industries for producing weaning foods
Appropriate Technology vol. 14 no. 2 1987

The Situm banana chip enterprise
Appropriate Technology vol. 11 no. 1 1984

Small-scale fruit processing in Saint Vincent
Appropriate Technology vol. 10 no. 2 1983

Recipes for independence
Appropriate Technology vol. 12 no. 1 1985

Leaf protein — a simple technology to improve nutrition
Appropriate Technology vol. 14 no. 2 1987

Improving the traditional Ghanaian baking oven
Appropriate Technology vol. 6 no. 2 1979

Cassava crispbread
Appropriate Technology vol. 12 no. 1 1985

Women and fish-smoking technology
Appropriate Technology vol. 14 no. 3 1987

Women and beekeeping
Appropriate Technology vol. 9 no. 3 1983

Small-scale expelling of sunflower seed oil
Appropriate Technology vol. 12 no. 1 1985

HD6073.F7 W65x   c.1
                                  100106 000
Women and the food cycle / int

3 9310 00083904 1
GOSHEN COLLEGE-GOOD LIBRARY